RICHMOND ESSENTIAL English

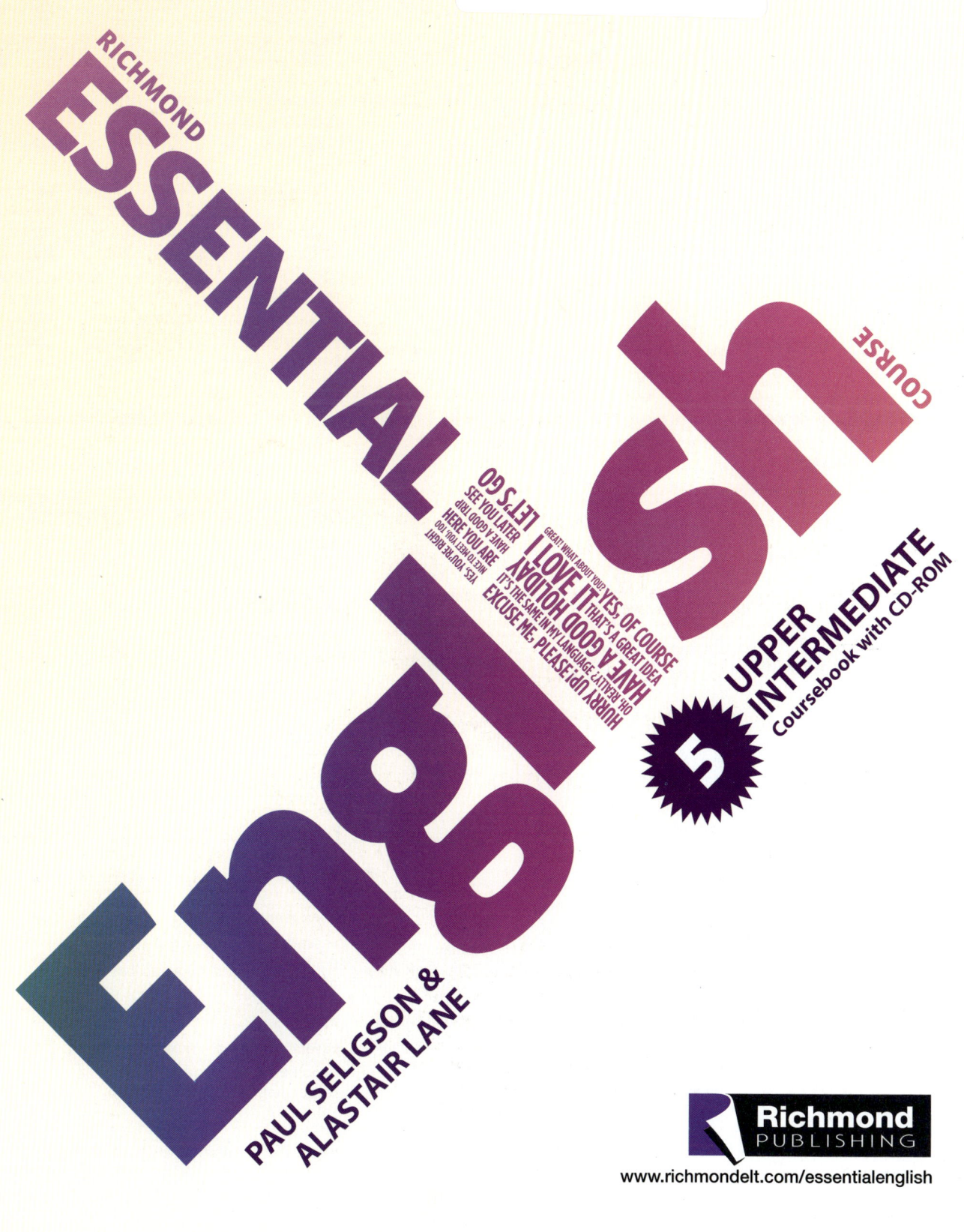

PAUL SELIGSON & ALASTAIR LANE

COURSE 5

UPPER INTERMEDIATE
Coursebook with CD-ROM

Richmond PUBLISHING

www.richmondelt.com/essentialenglish

Course book contents map

Unit 1

page	Lesson	Language in action	Grammar	Vocabulary	Pronunciation	Recycling
4	1A Life Crisis!	I thought I'd walk into a well-paid job. It got her thinking.	Tense review (Past, Present and Future)	Work collocations Essential phrases: giving advice		Paraphrasing
6	1B Happy Families?	I take after my dad. You can look it up in the dictionary.	Phrasal verbs	Phrasal verbs for relationships	Stress in phrasal verbs	*none* v *no-one* Describing family
8	1C Life since Web 2.0	José felt really embarrassed. Then 3 strange men arrived.	Narrative tenses	Words for feelings	Unstressing auxiliary verbs The schwa	Talking about the net Storytelling The schwa
10	1D Trading places	She was slowly getting used to the cold. Finnish coffee is unbelievably strong.	*Be used to* *Get used to*	Intensifiers, e.g. *slowly, incredibly, unbelievably* Essential phrases: making suggestions	Homographs (words with same spelling and different pronunciation)	*Used to* Describing places Saying how you are Work and home life
12	1E The grass is always greener...	If you get to the airport on time the plane is always late. If I go outside, I'll freeze. If you were an actor, you'd have a very stressful life.	Zero conditional First conditional Second conditional *As* v *like*	Common sayings Collocations with *get*		Guessing meaning from context Paraphrasing
14	1F Going away	I'm having a party next Saturday. It starts at 9pm. Marc will turn up at 10. I'm not going to hang around.	Future forms (*will, going to*, Present Simple, Present Continuous)	Phrasal verbs Essential phrases: expressing preferences re travel	Linking sounds Understanding rapid speech	Talking about travel and journeys Present continuous = *going to* future

16 Revision 1   60 Writing 1: a formal email   75 Sounds chart: 12 vowels   77 Phrasebook 1   79–85 Activity Book   112 Essential Grammar 1

Unit 2

page	Lesson	Language in action	Grammar	Vocabulary	Pronunciation	Recycling
18	2A The first job I ever had was...	I enjoyed the film we watched last night. The only person online was Lee, who was answering emails.	Defining and non-defining relative clauses	Adjective suffixes (1) Noun + *-y*, adjective + *ish*	Tip: pausing	Jobs Adjectives to describe experiences
20	2B White lies	It's never OK to lie, is it? You don't tell lies, do you?	Question tags	Negative prefixes for confirming facts	Question tags for confirmation and real questions	*Let* Talking about past experience
22	2C Dress-down Friday	She told me she's going to Chile next week. They asked me when I was starting that job.	Reported speech Reported questions	Reporting verbs Essential phrases: reacting to ideas	Word stress	Clothes Likes and dislikes Imperatives
24	2D Cash on the side	He stopped to have a coffee. He stopped smoking last year.	Verb + infinitive and / or Verb + gerund	Money idioms Essential phrases: talking about spending habits	Word stress	Habits and routines Verbs of emotion
26	2E The shape of things to come	It will be 10 degrees warmer. By 2050 everybody will be reading electronic books. The population will have doubled.	Future Simple, Future Continuous, Future Perfect for predictions	Noun forms Essential phrases: making predictions	Word stress with suffix *-ic* Contractions	*Going to* for prediction
28	2F Testing times	It could have happened to anyone. He must have remembered me...	Past modals for speculation and obligation *What* + noun *How* + adjective	Parts of a car Essential phrases: building and responding to a story	Auxiliary verbs (*should / would / could have*)	Explaining a process Predicting

30 Revision 2   61 Writing 2: An anecdote   75: Sounds chart: 8 diphthongs   77 Phrasebook 2   86–92 Activity Book   114 Essential Grammar 2

Unit 3

page	Lesson	Language in action	Grammar	Vocabulary	Pronunciation	Recycling
32	3A I am what I am	Kim's at university in Geneva. I've got a new email. Dubai is in the UAE. There's a problem with the car.	Articles	Changing images and the media		Describing people *Remind* v *remember*
34	3B Man-flu	Could you help me? Do you know if there are any problems? Do you mind staying at a cheaper hotel?	Indirect questions	Illnesses Essential phrases: explaining lifestyles	Shadow reading Silent letters	Questions with *mind* Comparing men and women
36	3C The art of the street	I've sent over a hundred emails today. It's been raining for hours!	Present perfect simple vs Present perfect continuous	Busking and living statutes Word + preposition Essential phrases: saying what you've been doing		Non-action verbs Countable v uncountable nouns (*Few, a few, a couple of* etc.)
38	3D Changing times	I wish I had my own car. If only we'd had more time.	*Wish* and *if only*	The face and appearance	Unstressed words and sentence stress	Describing appearance Giving advice Past modals
40	3E Gadget mania	If you'd been there, you would have loved it. If I'd had more money, I could have bought that ring.	Third conditional	Describing objects and their function	Intonation and stress for emphasis	It's used for / It looks like *Made of* vs *made from*
42	3F Artist at work!	An exhibition was held in London. He taught Congo to paint.	More irregular past participles UK and US English	Describing pictures	Irregular past participles	Uses of *on* Irregular past verbs

44 Revision 3   62 Writing 3: A biography   75 Sounds: 9 unvoiced consonants   78 Phrasebook 3   93–99 Activity Book   116 Essential Grammar 3

Unit 4

page	Lesson	Language in action	Grammar	Vocabulary	Pronunciation	Recycling
46	4A Live: tonight!	She was going to come to lunch but she's changed her mind. The meeting was to start at 7pm. They were leaving later that afternoon.	The future in the past *Be (about) to…*	Concerts and gigs Essential phrases: talking about past experiences	Intonation for giving good or bad news	Questions that end in prepositions Future tenses
48	4B How technology can change your life	I've got very little free time now. There's plenty of milk. There were hardly any passengers on the train.	Quantifiers (*much, many, little, a few* etc.)	UK and US English *Be / keep in / lose touch with*		UK v US English spelling Countable / uncountable nouns
50	4C Any volunteers?	Many cheetahs are killed by hunters. Most meat is cooked before we eat it.	The passive	Charity and the environment Volunteering	Homophones (words with different spelling but same pronunciation)	Jobs
52	4D Reality TV ruined my life!	If I were a billionaire, I'd buy my own island.	Mixed conditionals	TV shows Pairs of adjectives Essential phrases: speculating about the past	Linking Sentence stress Schwa vowel	Paraphrasing idioms Second and third conditionals
54	4E My avatar and me	Bill is just as mad as his brother! My dad is much older than my mum.	Making comparisons	Internet services	Stress on *much, a lot, a bit,* etc.	Superlatives
56	4F The Internet generation	Although we didn't have any tickets, we went along anyway. Even though we are working incredibly hard we don't have much hope of success.	Linking phrases	Childhood activities Adjective suffixes (2)		Technology Apostrophes: *My brother's car is a Fiat.*

58 Revision 4   63 Writing 4: A review   75 Sounds: 15 unvoiced consonants   78 Phrasebook 4   100–106 Activity Book   118 Essential Grammar 4

64–76 Word Bank   107 Student's Book audioscript   110 Activity Book audioscript

1A Life crisis!

Speaking

1 In five minutes, find out as much as you can about the other students.

How long have you been learning English?

Reading

2 Read the introduction to a magazine article. In pairs, list five things you think might cause a 'Quarterlife Crisis'.

3 Quickly read the rest of the article. How many of your ideas does it mention?

4 Re-read the article and match headings a–e to paragraphs 1–5.

a Everyone is more successful than me!
b The experience trap.
c I want to be alone!
d Cash disappearing fast.
e Where is my life going?

5 **1.1** Can you express or exemplify the meaning of the yellow words in the text? Go to Word Bank 1, p. 64.

Oh no, it's the quarterlife crisis!

In recent years, people in their twenties have been suffering from more worry and stress than ever before. This has led to a new concept, *The Quarterlife Crisis*, a term coined by US author Abby Wilner. But what is it that they are so worried about?

1 _____

You stay at school until you're 18. Then you spend three or four years at university. You should walk straight into a top job: your own office, a big desk and a secretary ready to listen to your commands. Right? Er... not quite. For many young people, employers aren't interested in their qualifications unless they have experience too. You send out hundred of CVs. You apply for every job you see, but it's always the same. You need one to two years' experience to get a job, but you need a job to get the experience... So you'll probably have to do work experience – without getting paid!

2 _____

University is over and now is the time to move into your own apartment, and have your own home. Or is it? Housing costs have been rising year on year for over a decade and it's getting harder and harder to find somewhere affordable to live. Many people in their twenties have to rent or even share a room in someone else's house, or can't afford to leave home at all, so it's hard for them to have their own independence.

3 _____

At school and college, your life has a very clear path. You do a course, pass an exam and then get a grade. It's easy to see what kind of progress you have been making. In the adult world, however, it's easy for life to lose its direction, or to get stuck in a job you only took for the money. There's only so long that you can do a mindless job before you get sick to death of it!

4 _____

Everywhere you look: on TV, in glossy magazines, in films and adverts, you are surrounded by pictures of beautiful twentysomethings. They all have great jobs and live in amazing apartments in the city centre, while you are still the junior employee in a huge corporation, if you have a job at all. You feel like you're missing out on life, and that can put you under a lot of stress.

5 _____

Education costs money, and so does everything else. You need to buy clothes for work, clothes for going out, and all those 'must have' electrical gadgets. Once, a computer was a luxury, but nowadays a mobile phone and a laptop are essentials. And if you don't have a job, how can you pay for all these things? You have to borrow: and many people in their twenties are already heavily in debt.

Speaking

6 In fours, discuss questions 1 to 4 for 5 minutes.

1 Have you experienced any of the problems in the article?
2 Which problem is the biggest one?
3 Is there anything you disagree with?
4 Think of four useful things young people can do to combat stress and stop worrying.

Listening

7 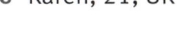 Listen to five people talking about the Quarterlife Crisis. Match their comments to paragraphs 1-5 in the article. Whose accent is most similar to yours?

a Anja, 20, Poland ☐
b Maria, 22, Argentina ☐
c Karen, 21, UK ☐
d Jelal, 21, Turkey ☐
e Bertil, 23, Holland ☐

> **Remember?**
> When we use *for / to*, *in / into* and *at / in*?

Grammar
Tense review

8 Go to audioscript 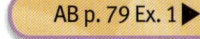 on page 107. Underline examples of:

a 2 different present tenses
b 4 different past tenses
c 2 different present perfect tenses.

9 Which tenses in ex 8 are simple and which are continuous?

10 In pairs, make an example sentence for each tense about one or both of you.

> Neither of us enjoys playing or watching football.

> Dani's only been living here since 2009.

AB p. 79 Ex. 1 ▶

Speaking

11 📄 In pairs, get a card from your teacher. Role-play the situations.

> **Essential phrases**
> You really should/ought to…
> In your case, I would…
> You could think about…
> One thing you could do is…
> Have you thought about + ing…?
> If I were you…
> Another possibility is to…

UNIT 1   5

1B Happy families?

Speaking

1 🔊1.3 Who in your family do you look like / take after? Go to Word Bank 2, p. 65.

I've got my Dad's ears and my Mum's temper.

2 In fours, answer the web quest survey. Any coincidences? Are you often asked to complete surveys like this?

None. I'm an only child.

Remember?
The difference between *none* and *no one*?

Family search

Hi! Can you spare 5 minutes to fill in our web quest on families around the world? Your answers could make a difference!

1. How many siblings have you got?
2. Who's your favourite family member?
3. Which member of your family do you speak to most often?
4. Do you have many uncles or aunts? Briefly describe one of them. What is he/she like?
5. Who are the oldest and youngest members of your family?
6. Have you got any in-laws? Do you get on well with them?

SUBMIT

Listening

3 You're going to hear four people describe the most annoying member of their family. Look at the pictures A–D. In pairs, guess what they'll say about each person.

4 🔊1.4 Listen and match the speakers to the pictures. Were your predictions accurate? What else did you manage to catch?

Zhu Zhu   Lisa   Claudia   Ben

5 Listen again. What's the relationship between each speaker and their family member? Who's the most annoying member of your family?

My grandparents really get on my nerves. Every time I see them, the first question they ask me is 'when are you getting married?'

Grammar

6 Match examples 1–4 with rules a–d.
1. I'm looking forward to meeting your new boyfriend.
2. If you don't know a word, you can look it up in the dictionary.
3. Sorry I'm late. My car broke down.
4. We get off the train at the next station.

7 Match the phrasal verbs in yellow 1–4 from audioscript 🔊1.4 on p. 107 with rules a–d.

A

B

C

D

Phrasal verbs

a. Separable PVs have an object which can go between the verb and particle (the particle is the word like *away*, *with*, *from*).
b. Inseparable PVs have an object which cannot go between the verb and particle.
c. Intransitive PVs have no object.
d. Three-part PVs have two particles. The PV cannot be separated.

▶ AB p. 80 Ex. 3

Pronunciation

8 (1.5) Complete 1–4 with these verbs. Listen, check and mark the sentence stress. Then circle the correct rule:

> take after   fall out
> grow up   get on

1 He wasn't like this when I _____.
2 We _____ over it all the time.
3 I had thought that they always _____ well together.
4 Well, I _____ my dad.

Rule: The stress in phrasal verbs is usually on *the verb itself / the particle*.

Reading

9 Read the introduction to an article about China. In pairs, answer these questions.

1 What do you think the title refers to?
2 What kind of family does the author have?
3 Why did the One Child Policy start and has it been successful?
4 Does it affect every Chinese family?
5 Imagine four effects the One Child Policy has had on China.

A billion to one

If you get on well with your siblings, they can be some of the best friends you have in your life, although it wasn't like that in my family because my sister was ten years older than me. She was like a third parent when we were young, constantly telling me off. We fell out all the time as children, although I think we're actually very similar because we both take after our mother.

I've been thinking about her more and more recently as I have been living and working in China, where the government has had the "One Child Policy" since 1979. To restrict population growth, they decided that families in urban areas could only have one child each. Now after thirty years of the policy in action, the Chinese government estimates that the country has had 400 million fewer births. But what effects has it had on everyday life?

10 Read the rest of the article. How exactly does the One Child Policy affect:
● children?   ● the possibilities for marriage?   ● older people?   ● women?

For many children, it has meant that they grow up in a world of adults and often feel lonely because there's no one else in the family to play with. As the only member of the new generation, ¹many children also find it hard to live up to all the expectations of older family members.

The problems don't stop there. When the One Child Policy was introduced, many more boys were born than girls. Families preferred to have boys because they could take care of relatives when they became elderly. Suddenly, there weren't enough girls around. This has led to a change to the law, called "the one and a half children policy". Now, couples in the countryside are allowed to have two children – ² as long as their first child is a girl.

At the other end of the spectrum, the policy has had further, unforeseen, consequences. ³China's population is greying fast. In the past, mothers used to have an average of five children each, but that figure has fallen to just two. As more and more people retire and stop work, there aren't enough young people to replace them. ⁴This creates a headache for the government, because they need lots of workers to keep the economy moving.

But if the government wants people to have more children, ⁵they may have a struggle on their hands. Many mothers are having fewer children not because of the One Child Policy, but because they cannot put up with the stress of looking after a large family. ⁶Working women have to juggle long working hours with family life. For many women, it just isn't possible to bring up lots of children as well as managing a full-time career.

11 In pairs, explain, exemplify or paraphrase the yellow phrases in the text.

Speaking

12 In threes, discuss these questions.

1 Does your country have any similar problems to the ones in the article?
2 What's the ideal number of children for a family nowadays?
3 If you could choose, for your 'next life' would you come back as an only child, the eldest or youngest child, and would you prefer to be a boy or a girl?

> We have the opposite problem. Our birth rate is falling.

UNIT 1   7

1C Life since Web 2.0

Speaking

1 **1.6** Quickly read the article. How has Web 2.0 changed your life? Are you surprised by how much you use it? Which websites are you keenest on? Go to Word Bank 3, p. 66.

2 The photos A–D all come from a website put together by a group of friends. Anyone in their group can access it to upload photos or write an entry. In pairs, imagine what's happening / been happening / going to happen in each photo?

A

August 1st

B

August 11th

C

August 19th

D

August 27th

When the Internet first became popular, users were just passive, as if they were going to a library. They accessed websites and read what was there. But since the introduction of Web 2.0 in 1999, that's all changed. Nowadays, over half the web is created by users themselves, and over 50% of web users are actively creating web content by writing texts (Wikipedia), blogs and messages (Twitter) and posting their own photos and videos (YouTube and Flickr). The fact is that now the Web belongs to us!

1 Post from Karen   6:15 p.m.

Here he is – Dieter! Martina's new boyfriend. I finally took their photo when they (1) *were staying* at my house last weekend. I knew they had been going out for ages and we had to pretend it was secret, but now everybody knows. She (2) *went red* when she realised that we all knew about it! She looks pretty happy now though, doesn't she? Mind you, so does he!

2 Post from Andrea   6:20 p.m.

Party!!! Julie is always moaning that no one ever celebrates her birthday because it's in the middle of summer! But she looks pretty happy here doesn't she? No one (3) *had told her* beforehand so she was a bit shocked when she came to my house and found everybody waiting for her! When everyone jumped out from where they (4) *had been hiding* she went white! He, he! Shame you couldn't join us, Mitch!

3 Post from Anna   6:22 p.m.

Sorry I didn't write sooner but the computers hadn't been working before today. I'm so jealous of you all! While you (5) *were travelling* round London or wandering round the mountains, I was slaving away in a holiday camp. The job is OK but I have to wake up at 6 a.m. every morning!! ☹ I'm sooooooo stressed out! Hope to see you all soon! Let's meet up as soon as summer's over!

4 Post from Carrie   6:25 p.m.

Who is that mysterious man in the canoe? Yes, Mitch finally convinced us to go on an adventure holiday with him. He'd been talking about a trip to the mountains for years so he was delighted when we finally did agree to go with him. Obviously, because it was his plan, he had to do all the work. (Note Becky in the right of the picture... not helping!)

5 Post from Paula   6:26 p.m.

OK, Anita and I look pretty happy in this photo but actually we were completely lost. We had been walking around London for TWO HOURS ☹ looking for our hostel before we eventually found it! We were exhausted! (Although we did stop for a bit of shopping on the way... of course!).

Reading

3 Match the website entries 1–5 with photos A–D. Which entry does not go with any of the photos?

4 In pairs, answer the questions. Who...
1. had been surprised by their friends?
2. was very tired after they had been travelling?
3. had missed a party?
4. was embarrassed?
5. was fed up?
6. was feeling very happy after everyone agreed to a plan?
7. was working very hard?

Grammar

5 Look at yellow phrases 1–5. Match them to rules a–e in the grammar box below.

> **Narrative tenses**
> a The most common past tense is the Past Simple. It is used for finished past actions.
> b Use the Past Continuous to describe an action that begins, and possibly finishes, after another past action.
> c Use the Past Continuous to describe actions in progress at a point in the past.
> d Use the Past Perfect to describe actions happening before another past action.
> e Use the Past Perfect Continuous to emphasise that the previous action is in progress over a period of time.

6 Now find one example of the Past Perfect Continuous in each post on p. 8. Could you use the Past Perfect in these cases too? Why? Why not?

AB p. 81. Ex. 5 ▶

> **Tip**
> In ⊕ sentences, the auxiliary verbs *do* and *did* are often used to emphasise the verb.
> We **did** stop for a bit of shopping.
> I **do** know how to use the dishwasher, thanks!

Listening

7 1.7 Some of the friends from the website went on holiday together. Listen to Martina and José. After each pause, guess what they will say next. Was it a success? How do you think the story ends?

8 Listen and order the story 1–7. Which event is <u>not</u> mentioned by José?
- a ☐ They went walking in the mountains.
- b ☐ They ate bread and cheese.
- c ☐ Mitch booked the accommodation on the Internet.
- d ☐ José felt really embarrassed.
- e ☐ *1* They went canoeing.
- f ☐ They arrived at an empty house.
- g ☐ Everyone was feeling really down.
- h ☐ Three strange men arrived.

Pronunciation

9 1.8 Auxiliary verbs are usually unstressed and pronounced /ə/, which makes them difficult to hear. Listen again to six sentences. How many words do you hear?

a ☐ b ☐ c ☐ d ☐ e ☐ f ☐

10 In pairs, look at audioscript 1.8 on page 107. Practise saying the sentences quickly, using the schwa /ə/ (but never stress it).

> **Remember?**
> The schwa /ə/ is the most common sound in English. About ⅓ of unstressed vowel sounds are pronounced /ə/.

Speaking

11 In pairs. Take a card from your teacher. They show the end of the story (the next day). Can you tell the rest of the story using narrative tenses?

UNIT 1   9

1D Trading places

Speaking

1 What do these things have in common? What do you know about them?

> That's a reindeer.

2 (1.9) Have you ever been anywhere incredibly cold or unbelievably expensive? Tell your partner. Go to Word Bank 4, p.66.

Reading

3 Scan Gemma's blog for two minutes. In pairs, remember two things she says about:

| herself | the weather | her boyfriend | Helsinki | the Finnish language | food and drink | the sauna |

Hi! I'm Gemma McGoohan, an Australian living in Finland. Welcome to my blog.

F-f-fabulous F-F-F-Finland!

After I'd been in Helsinki about a month, I saw something incredible. I **immediately** rushed home to tell my Finnish boyfriend the news. "Timo! You wouldn't believe it! The sea's frozen! Totally. The whole sea!!"

Timo didn't even look up from his newspaper. "Yeah, yeah. It does that every year" he said. He was clearly less impressed than me. But what do you expect? I'm from Perth in Western Australia and I'd never even seen snow before. I was only slowly getting used to the cold, and now the sea was a solid block of ice. It was **absolutely** amazing!

Timo might sound like a man of few words, but **actually** most Finnish people are like that.

Like the metro in the morning – it's **totally** silent. I'm used to the quiet now but I found it pretty weird when I first arrived.

Finns are also not exactly talkative. I've got used to having **incredibly** short conversations. For example, back home, you'd start the day something like this:

"Hi Gemma. How's it going?"

"Good, thanks. How was your night?"

"Yeah, it was great thanks, **really** good..." And the conversation would go on like this for about ten minutes. But here, the equivalent conversation consists of one word: "Moi." The reply is "Moi". And that's the end. Period. I used to start every day chatting to everyone at work, but now, I just say "moi" like everybody else!

"Moi" is a really useful word for me, because learning Finnish has been really tough. The pronunciation is **completely** impossible. Nobody understands me when I say "Puhutteko englantilainen?" – "Do you speak English?" – I have to say it *in* English.

There have been a couple of other surprises too. The coffee is one. The Finns drink the most coffee in Europe, and it's **unbelievably** strong. If you drink half a cup for breakfast, you'll be up all night!

The other surprise has been lunchtime. People eat lunch **ridiculously** early: 11 am isn't uncommon! It's because people often arrive at their offices at 7 am, so by late morning, they're starving. I'm used to eating lunch a bit later so I'm still having problems with that.

I have to mention the most famous thing from Finland – the sauna! Well, I've saved the best for last. Timo took me to one in my first week, when it was freezing outside, and it was one of the greatest experiences of my life! Awesome! It was an **extremely** cold day and the heat in the sauna was amazing! I remember sitting there, feeling like a princess, thinking, "Yes, I could **really** get used to this!"

Anyway, more news from my 'F' blog next month!

1D

4 Re-read the text. Which of the yellow words do you use a lot in your own English?

> **Remember?**
> Six ways to respond to *How are you doing?* or *How's it going?*

Grammar

5 Look at the underlined words in the text. Complete the rules with *used to*, *be used to* or *get used to*.

> **Be used to / get used to**
>
> _____ is a verb describing habits in the past. However, it can also be used after *be* and *get*.
>
> _____ means something is already familiar for the speaker.
>
> _____ means something is becoming familiar.
>
> *Be / Get used to* is followed by a noun or verb + *-ing*.

> AB p. 82 Ex. 4 ▶

6 Has your work/home life changed in the last year? Is there anything that you aren't used to, or are getting used to?

> *I'm slowly getting used to doing homework again.*

Listening

7 (1.10) Listen to four people who are living abroad. Where are they originally from? Which countries do they live in now?

Anna   Bruno   Otis   Tessa

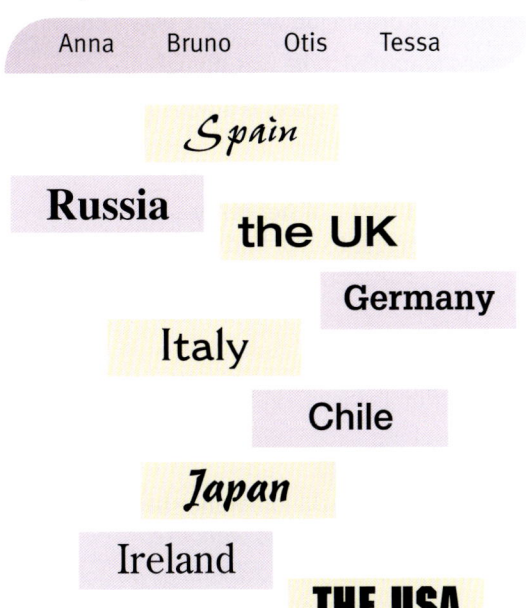

Spain
Russia
the UK
Germany
Italy
Chile
Japan
Ireland
THE USA

8 Listen again. Answer the questions.
1. What was the problem with public transport for Anna?
2. Why didn't Bruno like the food?
3. What's wrong with Otis' workplace?
4. What change does Tessa talk about?
5. Each speaker discussed a problem. Have they got used to the problem now?

Pronunciation

9 (1.11) A small group of words in English are spelt the same but pronounced differently. In pairs, how do you pronounce the words in pink? Listen and check. Do you know any others?

1. a We used trams to get around Dublin.
   b He's not used to eating spicy food.
2. a I usually read the paper on my way to work.
   b I read a really good book while I was on holiday.
3. a We need someone to lead the jungle expedition.
   b X-rays cannot move through lead.
4. a You're standing too close to me!
   b Can you close the door please?
5. a Mike has had a huge row with his grandmother and now they're not talking to each other!
   b We'll be waiting on the row of seats outside the station.

Speaking

10 Imagine a British friend is coming to live in your country. Think of 6 key tips to help him / her prepare for the experience.

> *In my country, you need to get used to going out late. We don't usually meet up with friends until after 11 pm!*

Essential phrases

I would recommend…
You need to think about…
One of the good things is… but, on the other hand, one of the bad things is…
One problem you might come up against is…
A lot of visitors find our…

Unit 1   11

1E The grass is always greener…

Speaking

1 In groups, read these common sayings. Do you know what they mean? Do you have similar expressions in your language?

"The grass is always greener on the other side."

"You can lead a horse to water, but you can't make it drink."

"Two's company, three's a crowd."

"A change is as good as a rest."

"It never rains but it pours."

2 In pairs, think of a situation when you could use these sayings.

A: *I downloaded lots of job adverts from the Internet and I showed them to Dmitri, but he didn't apply to any of them.*
B: *Well, you can lead a horse to water but you can't make it drink.*

Listening

Mauro Vazzoler's 24 and a businessman from Argentina. In his work, he gets to travel worldwide, arranging events and parties for celebrities and famous people.

3 (1.12) In pairs, imagine three interesting things that Mauro gets to do in his job. Word Bank 1, p. 64.

It must be great getting the chance to travel so much.

4 (1.13) Mauro's talking to a colleague, Nancy Harper. In pairs, Ⓐ listen and answer questions 1–3. Ⓑ listen, read the script on page 107 and check Ⓐ's answers.

1 What are Mauro and Nancy doing?
2 What does Mauro say about his job?
3 Who's Vanessa? What's she doing at the moment?

5 (1.14) Listen to part 2 of the conversation, Swap roles. Ⓑ listen and answer. Ⓐ listen, read page 107 and check.

1 What was Nancy's dream job when she was a child?
2 What job does Mauro wish he was doing?
3 Why does Nancy say "the grass is always greener"?

Reading

6 Mauro e-mailed Vanessa to ask her about life as an actor. In pairs, Ⓐ, read Part 1 of her reply on p. 13. Ⓑ, read Part 2. Then answer the questions together. Would you prefer to live and work like Mauro or like Vanessa?

1 Where's Vanessa at the moment?
2 How do most actors spend their working lives?
3 What part of her life outside of work makes Vanessa unhappy?
4 What does she think about Mauro's job?
5 What does she recommend Mauro to do?
6 What happened to the other students on her course?

7 In pairs, explain, define or exemplify the yellow words in the text.
For example: Don't worry, Jan's got plenty of money!

Tip

Note the difference between *work as* and *work like*.

Now she's working as an actor!
I've been working like a madwoman!

12

Part 1

Hi Mauro

Great to hear from you! I'm writing this from a café in Minnesota. It's got WiFi and plenty of coffee so I'm pretty happy here. In fact, I don't want to leave, because I know that if I go outside, I'll freeze! It's −10° today! I'm so jealous of you working in South Africa. I can only dream of heat like that at the moment.

How funny that you are thinking of acting again! I was just thinking how good your life sounds now! A regular income, international travel, lots of paid holidays. If I were you, I wouldn't give that up!

I mean, making a living from acting is so hard! You know, after drama school, I reckon about half of my class never worked in acting. It's just too scary. You never know if you'll have work from one day to the next. It's incredibly difficult to get your first job too, because you need an agent. But none of the good agents are interested in new actors.

Part 2

OK, it's true that I've got this job in the USA. But I was lucky because my mum's American, so it was easy for me to get a work visa. But don't forget that 90% of actors are resting 90% of the time!

Another thing is that I have no home life at all, because we're always working evenings and weekends. I'm living out of a suitcase and I've been working like a madwoman! I know you travel a lot too, but at least you get to go home sometimes!

Anyway, if you really want more information about acting as a career, I'll send you some. But my advice is to stay put.

We should meet up soon. I'm coming back to the UK in March and if I find a cheap flight, I'll come over and visit you in Milan. I need a holiday like crazy!

Take care.

Love,
Vanessa

Grammar

8 Correct these mistakes.

1 If I am Mauro, I wouldn't change my job.
2 If you spoke to Vanessa, she will tell you about working as an actor.
3 If there will be bad weather, the planes don't leave the airport.

9 Complete the rules for conditionals with *Present Simple*, *will*, and *would*. Then match the sentence halves.

Conditionals

The zero conditional *If* + Present Simple, _____
The first conditional *If* + Present Simple, _____
The second conditional *If* + Past Simple, _____

1 Use the zero conditional for — hypothetical situations.
2 Use the 1st conditional for — things which are always true.
3 Use the 2nd conditional for — realistic possibilities.

Remember?

You can use

*if I / he / she / it **were*** or *If I / he / she / it **was***

in speaking.

10 Name the conditionals in the yellow sentences in audio script 1.13 on page 107.

AB p. 83 Ex. 3 ▶

Speaking

11 In pairs, each make true sentences, 1–6. Compare ideas and add details. Talk for a minute about each one. Then share any good stories with the class.

1 If I go to the town centre at the weekend, I…
2 If I don't come to the next English class,…
3 If I go out with some friends tonight,…
4 When I was a child, I always wanted to be a _____ . If I were a _____ now,…
5 If I had more time/money, I…
6 If I were world famous, my life would be different because…

1F Going away

Speaking

1 In fours, answer the questions and compare your travel experiences.

1 How many countries have you been to? Which was the biggest / smallest?

2 What's the longest you've spent away from home? Why?

Actually, I've never been abroad.

3 Do you remember much about your first big trip? How did you feel?

4 What's the furthest you've travelled: north, south, east and west?

Reading

2 🔵1.15 Paraphrase the nine phrasal verbs in the quiz below. Go to Word Bank 2 on page 65. Then, in pairs, answer the quiz.

What kind of traveller are you?

1 You're getting ready for a holiday abroad. What kind of clothes are you going to pack?

a I'll pack special clothes for the holiday: some good shirts and a new hat. If I run out of clothes while I'm away, I'll just buy some T-shirts with the name of the place on them.

b I won't change my look much. I'll just wear the same clothes as I do at home.

c I want to fit in with the locals so I'll find out what they wear and then pack similar clothes.

2 You're going to a country whose language you don't speak. What are you going to do?

a I'll just learn a few words of the local language like 'hello' and 'thank you' and take a phrase book too. I'm sure I'll get by.

b I'll just mime or speak English because everyone understands it.

c I'll use all available online resources and try to learn as many words as I can before I go.

3 You want to travel all around the country when you're there. What preparations are you going to make?

a I'll figure out everything I want to do. Then, I'll book all the tickets online before I go. I'm not going to hang around in railway stations waiting for trains!

b None. I'll make all the decisions when I get there. I'll just see what turns up.

c I'll have a look in the guidebooks and ask my friends for advice. If I need to arrange anything in particular, I'll do that before I go.

4 How do you decide what you're going to see during the trip?

a I'll make a decision after I check into the hotel.

b I'll call up everyone I know for suggestions. I'll also see if my friends know people in the country who can show me the places tourists never see.

c I'll do the main touristy things, and visit all the most famous museums.

5 You're going to a country with very different cuisine to yours. How are you going to decide what to eat?

a I'll look at all the food websites to find out the local delicacies and then I'll book the most famous restaurants so that I can try them all.

b I'll find out the areas where the main restaurants are and then, when I eat out in the evenings, I'll go there.

c I'll see when I get there. If I can't find somewhere good to eat, I'll just go to a fast food outlet or somewhere like that.

3 Work out your total and check what it means in the key on page 15. Do you agree with your profile?

14

Listening

4 🔊1.16 Kate's going to do a summer job in Athens. She's talking to Nick, who has lived in Greece for years. Listen. True (T) or false (F)?

1 Kate has lived abroad in three different countries.
2 Nick came to Athens before the Olympic Games.
3 Athens is really noisy at the moment.
4 Nick has arranged a coach tour of the city.
5 Kate is going to live on the island of Paros.
6 There are very few tickets available for the ferries.

> **Tip**
> To react quickly to news or a suggestion, use *(That) sounds* + adjective.
>
> *He's going to show us the sights.*
> *Sounds lovely.*

Grammar

5 Look at the yellow texts in audioscript 1.16 on page 107. Match them to rules 1–4.

> **The future**
> 1 *Will* can be used to describe a future fact or to make a prediction. It's not usually used to describe future arrangements.
> 2 Use *going to* for predictions and future plans and arrangements.
> 3 Use the *Present Continuous* for future plans and arrangements, e.g. things you'd write in a diary.
> 4 Use the *Present Simple* for timetabled events and schedules.

6 Look back at *What kind of traveller are you?* on p. 14. What verb form is used for the questions? And for the answers? Why?

> **Remember?**
> The Present Continuous for the future and *going to* are very similar. Both can be used to talk about future plans, especially when the plans have been made with other people.
>
> *I'm going to have tea with Angie on Monday.*
> *I'm having tea with Angie on Monday.*

AB p. 84 Ex. 3 ▶

Pronunciation

7 🔊1.17 Listen to these sentences from ex 4. What do you notice about the words in pink?

1 That's what I want to ask you.
2 So what are we going to do in Athens?
3 Well, don't get a ticket until you're in Athens.

8 🔊1.18 In speech, we sometimes add an extra sound to link vowel sounds: /w/, /j/ or /r/). Which linking sound connects the underlined words?

1 That's whY I phoned yoU Up.
2 I'm meeting yoU At thE Airport.
3 Athens is much moRE URban.

9 In pairs, practise saying the sentences in 7 and 8 quickly. Who can say them the fastest?

Speaking

10 📄 In threes, get a card from your teacher. Role-play the conversation at the travel agent's.

> **Essential phrases**
> I'm not very fond of…
> I'm not a fan of… / I can't stand…
> Personally, I'd rather…
> What I really want to do is…
> Have you considered…
> There are a number of things you could do…

Calculate your score for the quiz.

1 a = 1 b = 2 c = 3   2 a = 2 b = 1 c = 3
3 a = 3 b = 1 c = 2   4 a = 1 b = 3 c = 2
5 a = 3 b = 2 c = 1

Total:

5–7 points It sounds like you're a pretty adventurous traveller, or maybe you're just very relaxed. But it wouldn't hurt to do a little more preparation before you go away. The best holiday for you would be backpacking round the world.

8–11 points You're a pretty normal traveller. You make some plans but also like to take things as they come. Nobody wants to plan everything on holiday, do they? The best holiday for you is one where you book your hotels and flights before you leave, but do everything yourself online.

12–15 points You're a very careful traveller and always try to know everything before going away. But you might be a little too cautious – perhaps you could be a bit more spontaneous on holidays? The best holiday for you is a coach tour where the itinerary is organized in advance.

Revision

1 In pairs, ask and answer. Each / = 1 missing word. Any real surprises?

1 What / / find most difficult in English?
2 Why / / studying English / the moment?
3 When / / start / English properly?
4 /were / doing / you decided / do this course?
5 / / met anybody from this class before / began / course?
6 / many English teachers / / had? All female? What nationalities?
7 Have / / studying English a lot / class recently?
8 How / / / to use your English most / the future?

2 Name the tenses in questions 1–8.

3 Play STICK THEM TOGETHER. Get a card from your teacher.

4 In pairs, ask and answer. Any big differences between you?

1 Have you ever fallen out with someone in your family?

2 Where did you grow up?

3 Did you get told off a lot when you were a child? Who by?

4 What's the best place in your country to bring up children?

5 How old are most people in your country when they move out of their family home?

6 Which member of your family do you get on best/worst with?

7 Guess the three most common reasons why couples break up?

8 Do you take more after your mother or your father in looks/personality?

9 Did your family have high expectations that you needed to live up to?

5 Put the adjectives on page 66, Word Bank 3 into groups of 1, 2 or 3 syllables. Listen to 1.6 again to check.

6 1.19 James has just had a Turkish bath in Istanbul. Listen to him and his friend Mehmet. Complete the sentences.

1 James went to the baths on _____.
2 He couldn't go to the bath that Mehmet recommended because _____.
3 In the hamam, everyone stared at James because _____.
4 James was told off for putting _____.
5 James was impressed by _____.
6 Next time, Mehmet offers to _____.

Listen again to check.

7 1.20 Listen again and underline the stressed words. The number of stressed words is in brackets ( ).

1 Did you take my advice and visit the hamam, the Turkish baths? (3)
2 Did you go to a good one? (2)
3 Ah – maybe that's because you're a foreigner. (2)
4 But that's not right! (2)
5 But did you enjoy the hamam in the end? (3)
6 Next time you go to the baths, I'll go with you and I'll show you what to do. (4)

8 Make true sentences. In pairs, compare ideas. How many are the same?

Travelling by bus here is cheap but can be extremely slow.

1 _____
totally pointless!

2 _____
unbelievably cold!

3 _____
completely impossible!

4 _____
absolutely amazing!

5 _____
incredibly beautiful!

6 _____
extremely uncomfortable!

7 _____
ridiculously expensive!

9 Get a card from your teacher. Role-play a phone-call.

10 Match comments 1–6 with replies a–f. Add the missing word to each reply.

1 I think I'm the worst player on the team. I just can't run around anymore.
2 What time are we leaving?
3 I really need to find work during the summer holidays.
4 Timo's in bed, sneezing and coughing.
5 Did you enjoy the exhibition?
6 Is this a photo of you and Michael Schumacher?

a Then I won't come round today. I don't want get the flu.
b The best way get a job is through people you know.
c Yes, and no. There were glass cases around everything so I couldn't near any of the pictures.
d Right now! We need get going!
e Yeah. I get meet quite a lot of famous people in my job.
f Well, you're not any younger.

11 In pairs, think of five ways to complete the man's sentence.

12 Do ex 3 on p. 65.

13 In pairs, choose a topic and take turns to talk non-stop about each for one minute.

Something I'm worried about at the moment
Somebody I love talking to
How I use the Internet
My family home
Three things I like most about my country
A job I'd love to have
How I use my mobile
My ideal evening in
Something I'm fed up with
A good place to eat out
Something you find nerve-wracking
The day I moved out / will move out of home

14 Go to Word Bank 20 p. 75. Listen and chant the 12 vowel sounds.

Song: I still haven't found what I'm looking for by U2

To find the words, google *lyric* + the song title.

To find the video, google *video* + the song title and singer.

Go to Writing 1 p. 60

2A The first job I ever had was…

1 In pairs, read the sentences and mark them A if they come from job adverts, or E if they're from emails.

1 They're really selfish because they keep all the tips and don't share them with the rest of the staff. ☹ **E**

2 The company is responsible for a number of noteworthy developments in cold and flu prevention.

3 The management were furious when they saw how much petrol we had used last month.

4 The boss keeps complaining because we're useless at folding clothes.

5 Needed: an imaginative and creative person with excellent drawing and design skills

6 Flexible working hours: you must be ready to distribute flyers and promotional materials day or night.

7 Although it was extremely tough at first, I'm pretty comfortable in the classroom now.

2 **2.1** What are the seven jobs in ex 1? Go to Word Bank 5, p. 67.

Reading

3 In pairs, read an interview with Karl-Heinz Hoffmann about his first job. Ⓐ read Part 1. Ⓑ read Part 2. Then share your information. What does he say about these things?

A: his job now	home town
the factory	journey to work
pollution	

B: where he worked	washing
what he did at work	his boss
plastic objects	

4 Re-read the whole interview. Write the missing questions 1–7.

Part 1

Careers weekly

Next in our series on people's first jobs around the EU, we speak to Karl-Heinz Hoffmann, 27 from Nuremberg, whose first job was a little unusual….

1 _____

I'm working as a tour guide. I like it because I always wanted a job where I could walk about in the open air and talk to people. Nuremburg is also quite a touristy area, with plenty of noteworthy buildings so it's not a very difficult job.

2 _____

That is the question. In my first job, I worked for a factory that made black.

3 _____

It made black, the colour black. I didn't understand it when I started working there either. Basically, everything which is made of plastic or rubber has an artificial colour. And one of the most popular colours for car tyres and things like that is black. To make this colour, you need to burn coal, lots of coal, which creates carbon black. That's what the factory made.

4 _____

Not at all, it was awful. Every day would begin the same way. I would get off the train at the same station, which was always totally deserted. Then I had to walk through these streets and fields where everything was black. The environmental impact was clear to see. The local people were furious about it. I remember one morning when it was very icy, and even the snow was black. A cat ran past me which was once white, but was now… well, you know.

Part 2

It was no better in the office. If you touched something, anything, like a plant or a window, you would be covered in black dust. To wash it off, you had to use a special soap which ruined your skin. It did get rid of the colour though. I don't think it was dangerous but it wasn't nice at all.

5 _____

I did the work that nobody else wanted to do: photocopying, answering the phones, things like that. It was so repetitive. The best time of day was the afternoon when everyone else was in meetings. I used to sit at my desk and study for my university exams!

6 _____

I had a boss who was from the USA and we got on really well. She was really professional and taught me a lot about working in business. She was nice when I left the company too. She bought me a great English dictionary, which I still have. It's been really useful.

7 _____

I've never forgotten it. I often pick up a piece of black plastic, like a stapler or a ruler, and I remember the reason why it is that colour. It's amazing how many things in life are made in this invisible way.

Grammar

5 Study the yellow sentences in the text. Complete the Grammar box.

Relative clauses

1 A relative clause gives more information about a noun.
There are two types:
A *defining relative clause* tells you exactly what something is.
A *non-defining relative clause* gives you extra information about something. The clause is separated from the noun by a comma (,).

2 Use _____ to describe people, and _____ for things. Both may be replaced with *that*.
Use _____ to describe possession.
Use *why* to explain reasons.
Use _____ for time and _____ for location.

6 Find one example of a defining and non-defining relative clause in paragraph 6 of the text.

7 <u>Underline</u> six more relative clauses in the *Careers weekly* text.

Tip

When speaking, pause briefly before <u>and</u> after a non-defining relative clause.

AB p. 86 Ex. 4 ▶

Listening

8 2.2 Listen to Tsveti Bogdanova. What exactly did she have to do in her first job and why did she leave?

9 Listen again. What does Tsveti describe with these adjectives?

dependent	hellish	endless
automatic	trustworthy	repetitive
careful	messy	eggy	dangerous
professional	unforgettable

Tip

In speaking, add *–y* to a noun, or *-ish* to an adjective or to a time to mean *like* or *about*.
I think the cake is a bit too chocolatey.
See you at 6-ish.
She's got reddish hair.

Speaking

10 In fours, answer the questionnaire. If you've never worked, answer for a friend. Who has done the most unusual job in your group?

I used to deliver newspapers on Sundays when I was 12.

Work questionnaire

1 What was the first job you ever had? Did you enjoy it?
2 How many different jobs have you done?
3 Have you ever worked…
  • outdoors?
  • in an office?
  • for free?
  • in a service industry (waiter, receptionist, etc.)?
  • at night?

2B White lies

Reading

1 2.3 – 2.4 Is it always best to tell the whole truth? Is it ever OK to be dishonest or tell a white lie? Go to Word Bank 6, p. 68.

> *There are times when I'd avoid telling the truth.*

2 In pairs, read answers 1–6. Do you think their actions were right or wrong?

Is honesty the best policy?

Our readers told us about a time when they were dishonest (or just unwilling to tell the truth). Here are the top 6 replies. Do you think they did the right thing?

1. We were at a theme park and I couldn't find anywhere to park. The kids were getting really impatient and fighting, so I just put the car in a disabled parking space. That isn't immoral, is it?

2. The vet told me that our family hamster was very ill and would soon die. My four-year-old asked me if the hamster would be OK, and I said 'yes'. I don't think that was irresponsible. Everyone does it, don't they?

3. In the job interview, they asked me 'Do you speak good German?' Well, I had very basic school German so I said 'yes', and I got the job. It's OK. I thought the language skills were irrelevant, and they were, weren't they?

4. We were going to a nightclub and I was the only one who was underage. They asked me how old I was and I said '21' so luckily they let me in. It's OK. It wasn't illegal, was it?

5. The museum gave free entry to students so I showed them an illegible old photocopy of a letter that said I was at university and they let me in for free. It saved me €10!

6. My grandma cooked us liver and onions. It was completely inedible but when she asked what we thought, I said it was delicious! I didn't want her to feel disappointed.

Remember?
Let means allow or give permission:
The teacher let us go home early.

Grammar

3 <u>Underline</u> the four question tags in 2. Read the rule and complete the table.

Question tags

Use *auxiliary verb* + noun. If the statement is ⊕, the tag is ⊖ and vice versa.

Positive statement →	negative tag	Negative statement →	positive tag
I'm the only student	aren't I?	They aren't here,	_____?
You live there,	_____?	You don't live there,	_____?
You spoke to Mark,	_____?	We didn't finish,	_____?
They've gone home,	_____?	I've not met Jo,	_____?
He'll come to the party,	_____?	They won't complain,	_____?

AB p. 87 Ex. 3 ▶

Tip
The ⊖ question tag for *I am* is irregular.
I'm coming to your house tomorrow, aren't I?

Listening

4 (2.5) Listeners to a phone-in show were asked to comment on the lies in ex 2. Listen. Which lie is each person discussing? Do they approve of the lie?

1 Palat   2 Salvador   3 Judy

Pronunciation

5 (2.6) Listen again to four question tags. Write A (asking for agreement) or Q (real question). When does the intonation go up ↗ / down ↘?

1 Lying is always a bad thing, isn't it?
2 If lots of people pretend to be students, organisations will stop giving us discounts, won't they?
3 If someone takes the disabled parking space, we can't get into the building, can we?
4 I'm talking to James Richard's radio show, aren't I?

6 In pairs, practise 1–4. A say it, B say if it goes up or down. Swap roles.

Listening

7 You're going to listen to another extract from the radio show. In pairs, look at these pictures of people lying. Can you find 7 ways to spot a liar?

8 (2.7) Listen to the start of the radio show to check your answers. How many lies did you spot?

9 (2.8) Listen to the second part of the interview. Did you spot all seven ways to spot a liar?

10 (2.9) Listen to the final part of the interview. Ⓐ write down what Françoise says about the voice. Ⓑ write down George's experiment. Then compare your information.

Speaking

11 Write six facts about yourself. One or two of the facts must be false. In fours, tell each other your facts. Ask questions to find out which facts are lies. Can you spot the lie, using the experts' advice from the show?

A *I went to Egypt last year.*
B *Did you? Where exactly did you go?*
C *So, what currency do they use in Egypt?*

Essential phrases

Are you absolutely sure about that?

Really? Tell me a bit more about…

Can I just check something? You said…

That's a lie!

2C Dress-down Friday

Speaking

1. **2.10** In pairs, say what your favourite item of clothing is and why. Report back to the class. Go to Word Bank 7, p. 68.

   My hand-made leather boots.

2. Think of at least 6 jobs where people have to wear special clothing. Have you ever had to wear a uniform or other special clothing?

Reading

3. Look at the photo and answer the question in the article title. Imagine three ideas you'll find in the text. Then read it to check if they're there.

Shorts suits: Would you wear this to work?

As we are told that the men's 'shorts suit' is a key look for the office this summer, Robert Colvile bares his knees and sets off for the office.

'Are you sure you've got the knees for this?" asked my colleague. (1) _____

My new approach to workwear began after I was informed this week that **the business suit is slowly dying**. (2) _____ If standards continue to fall, the once-compulsory dress code could be dead within a decade. But an alternative interpretation of officewear is rapidly becoming popular: the shorts suit.

"Shorts are becoming a natural summer staple for those who dress well in the city," says the latest issue of GQ magazine – which praised the shorts suit as "**a bold fashion statement that's totally tied to what's in this summer.**".

(3) _____ After a successful debut last year, Topman's jacket-and-shorts combinations are already flying off the shelves.

"Formalwear is a very strong influence on the catwalks at the moment, and that's working its way down to the high street," explains Marcus Rigg, Topman's formalwear designer.

"**Guys are tidying themselves up and taking more pride in what they're wearing**. In terms of shorts, there has been a lot more exposure in the media, so they're a lot more acceptable."

(4) _____ As I walk around the Telegraph offices in a £135 shorts suit in light check from Topman, enjoying the feeling of the air against my legs, there is a predictable reaction.

I decide to escape their laughter and take to the streets, where I am grateful for British reserve. (5) _____

I comfort myself with the thought that age is on my side. "**There are a lot of younger people who don't have our preconceptions about clothes**." points out Charlie Porter, GQ's associate editor.

Most of the men I talk to want to discuss the difficult issue of the socks. (6) _____ However, among the women, the problem is not the shorts suit or the socks but showing any leg at all.

"**Men never really look good in shorts**," complains one colleague. "They're just a bit… unfortunate."

"I don't think shorts have ever worked on a man," another replies, before she mentions, "except perhaps Daniel Craig emerging from the sea in *Casino Royale* …"

Glossary
- **GQ:** a men's fashion magazine
- **Topman:** a British clothes store for men
- **Telegraph:** a newspaper

4. Re-read the text and match sentences a–f to the gaps 1–6. Check in pairs, Do you agree with the comments in **bold**?

   a Not among my colleagues they're not.
   b Should they be knee-length, pulled up, or simply absent?
   c Shoppers on the high street seem to agree.
   d To be honest, I wasn't.
   e Most people don't even look at the buildings around them, let alone a stranger in a shorts suit.
   f Only 24 per cent of office workers are now required to wear one.

5. Look at the yellow reporting verbs. Are they reporting direct or indirect speech?

Listening

6 2.11 Many companies in the UK have a 'dress-down Friday': a day when everyone comes to work in casual clothes. Listen to four people talking. Who likes (✓) and who doesn't like (✗) it?

Terry ☐   Katarzyna ☐   Dinesh ☐   Lisse ☐

7 Who said what? In pairs, try to match phrases 1 to 6 to the speaker. Write T, K, D or L. Then listen again to check.

1 ☐ They asked us if we wanted to continue.
2 ☐ I asked my manager why I couldn't wear my normal work clothes.
3 ☐ They asked me whether I had had the day off.
4 ☐ He replied that we had to dress casually on Fridays.
5 ☐ I told her I was going to wear, you know, jeans, a jumper.
6 ☐ I told my boss I thought it wasn't a good idea.

Grammar

8 Read the grammar box and circle the correct rules.

Reported speech and reported questions

1 To report speech move the tense *back/forward* one step.
 'I don't like dress-down Friday.' → He said he didn't like it.

2 This doesn't always happen, when the comment still affects the present or the *past / future*.
 'I'm going to Chile next week.' → She told me she's going to Chile next week.

3 With reported questions, the word order *sometimes / never* changes.
 'When are you starting this job?' → They asked me when I was starting that job.

4 Use *if* or *what / whether* to report questions that expect the answer 'yes' or 'no'.
 'Have you met Carl?' → She asked whether I had met Carl.

5 Time and place words *(yesterday, this) can / never* change when you report at a different time or place.
 'He left yesterday.' → They said he had left the hotel the day before.

Remember?
Imperatives become infinitives in reported speech. Go home! → He told me to go home!

AB p. 88 Ex. 4 ▶

Speaking

9 Many companies have similar ideas to dress-down Fridays to make people more relaxed and creative. Rank these ideas from 1–4. Which is the best / worst idea?

"Photo Friday. On Fridays, everyone in the office brings in a photo from outside their work life and puts it on their desk. It can be fun to do this with pics of you as a baby."

"No-message Friday. Nobody can send or read emails or texts on Friday. Everybody spends more time talking to colleagues."

"Friday lunches. Everybody in the company or on a team goes out for lunch together every Friday."

"Be nice Friday. You have to give all of your colleagues a compliment the first time you see them."

Essential phrases

... is a really good idea.
... is a ridiculous suggestion.
... wouldn't work in my office because....
How would... work?

2D Cash on the side

Speaking

1 **2.12 – 2.13** Think of five ways people make extra cash. Have you ever done any of these things? Go to Word Bank 8, page 69.

> They babysit for friends in the evening after work.

> Some people even sell their hair!

Listening

2 **2.14** Listen to a radio programme on making money on the side. Which of ideas 1–5 are mentioned? Which suggestion is missing?

1 Looking after other people's pets
2 Selling things over the Internet
3 Pretending to be a customer to see if a shop's service is good or bad
4 Giving private classes
5 Using your car to promote products

3 Listen again and complete these sentences.

1 The advantage of being strong when walking dogs is...
2 People don't put their property on online auction sites because...
3 People who enjoy being mystery shoppers usually can't afford...
4 The disadvantage of putting advertising on your car is...

Reading

4 In pairs, **A** read tips 1–3, **B** read tips 4–6 of the magazine article. Think of one more way of saving money. Then tell your partner the three ideas from the article plus your own suggestion. Can you guess which one did not come from the article?

5 In pairs, answer the questions, according to the article.

1 What three things does the author think you shouldn't buy?
2 What two changes should you make to regular payments?
3 Which three places can you save money at?

Credit Crunch tips
How to save money without changing your lifestyle!

In these difficult times, we'd all like to spend a bit less whenever we can – so here are six easy ways to save.

1 I'll never forget buying a top brand pair of jeans and then seeing my best friend wearing identical jeans that she had bought for half the price! Why waste money on expensive brand name products? Buy clothes at cheaper stores and save, save, save!

2 With Internet shopping becoming more and more popular, we're paying by plastic more than ever before. If you use your credit card a lot, remember to pay off the balance at the end of every month and avoid paying expensive interest.

3 We all do it. It's 7 a.m. and it's cold and you stop to have a coffee on the way to work. But have you thought how much it costs over a year to get a takeaway coffee every day? Make your own at home or at work and save the café for Sunday.

4 Do you really need a contract with 200 minutes of talk time and several hundred texts a month? Why not change to pay as you go? You'll discover that if you do forget to top up your phone once in a while, well, it's no tragedy.

5 If you want to keep fit, go to the public pool and stop paying a subscription to your local sports club. Going to the public swimming pool is much cheaper and you won't be paying out €€€s every month.

6 Remember throwing away all that old technology? Having to give away your first mobile, computer, and that huge old TV? What a waste of money that was! So, why buy DVDs or even go to the cinema when you can borrow them for a fraction of the price? Personally, I hate buying DVDs because I rarely watch them more than once.

Grammar

6 Add the yellow verbs from audioscript 2.14 on page 108 to Part 1 of the grammar box.

> **Verb patterns**
>
> Certain verbs are always followed by *to* + verb, others by the gerund:
> a verb + infinitive   *expect to,* _____, _____, _____, _____, _____
> b verb + gerund   *keep,* _____, _____

7 Match the pairs of sentences from the Reading to descriptions a or b.

Some verbs can either be followed by the infinitive (*to go*) or the gerund (*going*). The meaning changes depending on the pattern.	
1 stop paying a subscription stop to have a coffee	a end an action b end an action because you want to start another one
2 forget buying forget to top up	a a memory of the past b a future action
3 remember to pay off remember going	a advice for the future b a memory of the past
Other important verbs include: *go on*, *regret* and *try*	

> **Tip**
> Most verbs of emotion are followed by *–ing*, except *like, love, hate* and *prefer*, which can be followed by both infinitive or the gerund.
> *I like going / to go to the cinema.*

8 Make four true sentences. Compare in pairs. Any coincidences?

1 I'll never forget…
2 I really regret…
3 I'd love to try…
4 After leaving school, I went on…

> AB p. 89 Ex. 4 ▶

Speaking

9 In threes, compare your weekly spending. Draw a pie chart if you want to. Are there any ways that you could save a little money?

A *I don't earn much and over half my salary goes on transport.*

B *I'm really lucky because my parents still support me, so I don't have to pay bills or rent.*

C *I guess I could save a bit if I didn't go out so often, but …*

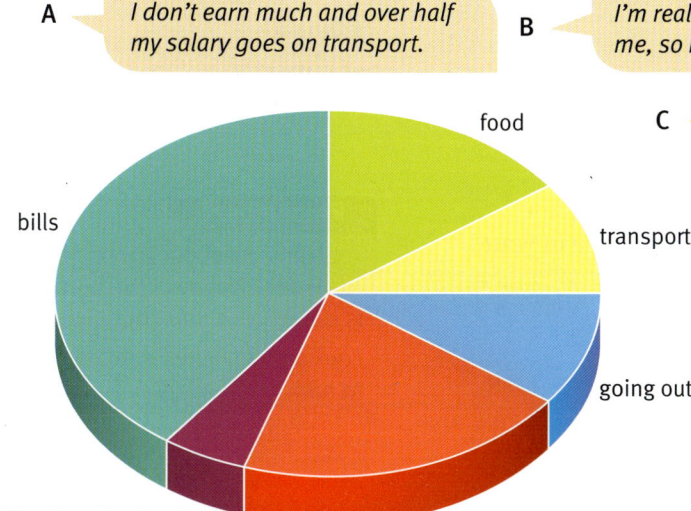

bills
food
transport
going out
clothes
DVDs, downloads, etc.

> **Essential phrases**
> I spend a lot of money on…
> In my country … is actually pretty cheap / ridiculously expensive
> I'm always buying…
> … costs / doesn't cost me a lot because…
> I guess I could give up…

2E The shape of things to come

Speaking

1 **2.15** Generally, are you optimistic or pessimistic about the future? Go to Word Bank 9, p. 69.

> *I'm usually optimistic about most things except global warming.*

2 In pairs, do the quiz. How confident are you that your answers are right?

> *We're fairly sure about all of them except...*

The 2050 Quiz

What **will the world be like** in the year 2050?
We asked the experts – can you guess their answers?

1 The present population of the earth is 6.7 billion. The United Nations say that by 2050, unless we take drastic action, the world's population...
   a **will have grown** to 9.2 billion.
   b will have doubled to 13.4 billion.

2 In 2050, **will we still be using** oil?
   a Yes, but several alternatives will have been discovered.
   b Yes, but reserves will be running out extremely fast.

3 Experts from Leeds University predict that if we don't take dramatic action now, how many animal and plant species **will have become extinct** by 2050?
   a 100,000   b 1,000,000

4 Most bananas in the world's supermarkets are actually the Cavendish banana. But in 2050, many people **won't be eating** them because...
   a they will have become allergic to bananas.
   b many of the banana plants will have been killed by a disease.

5 By 2050, what percentage of the world's population **will be using** English every day?
   a 50%   b 66%

3 **2.16** Listen and check. Do you agree with all five predictions? Write another prediction of your own for 2050.

By 2050, everybody will be reading electronic books.

Tip
We stress the syllable before *-ic*.
• allergic
• dramatic
• realistic

Grammar

4 Match the yellow examples in the quiz with each description, a–c. Then match a–c to the tense names. Which tense did you use in your prediction in ex 3?

Future: Simple, Continuous or Perfect for predictions
a Emphasises that an action will be finished before a point in the future.
b Predicts an action in progress at a point in the future.
c The standard tense used for making predictions.

Future simple ☐   Future continuous ☐   Future perfect ☐

Remember?
You can also predict with *going to*, especially when the prediction is based on a present situation.
Look at those clouds. It's going to rain.

AB p. 90 Ex. 3 ▶

26

Pronunciation

5 (2.17) Listen and repeat. Which sentence, *a* or *b*, sounds most natural? When would you use the pronunciation in the **a** sentences? Why?

1 a I will have it.   b I'll have it.
2 a We will be working.   b We'll be working.
3 a They will have done it.   b They'll have done it.

6 (2.18) Listen once to the dialogue. Who's talking? Did you understand every word they said?

7 Listen again line by line. In pairs, try to write down everything the speakers say. Then check your answers in the audioscript on page 108. Practise the dialogue at the same speed.

> **Tip**
> The Future Continuous is often used to speculate about what someone is doing at the moment of speaking.
> *Hurry up! I'm sure they'll be waiting for us outside the theatre.*

Speaking

8 In pairs, speculate about people you know. Any coincidences?

> *What do you think X will be doing now?*

Listening

9 (2.19) A *futurologist* is an expert who predicts what life will be like in the future. Listen and match four futurologists' predictions to a picture, A to D.

10 Listen again. Who's most optimistic and most pessimistic about the future? How do you know? Who do you agree with?

Speaking

11 In groups, make predictions about these things in 2050. Who's the optimist of your group? And the pessimist?

work   animal life   medicine   robots
homes   transport   weather   countries
languages   appearance and clothes

Essential phrases

I think that in the future…
Personally, I reckon…
I'm a bit of a pessimist / optimist because…
One of the biggest problems in the future will be…
I'm not sure about…

2F Testing times

Speaking

1 **2.20** In pairs, name 5 parts of a car. Go to Word Bank 10, p. 70.

the windows, the roof

2 What happens in a driving test in your country? Explain it to your partner.

First of all you have to do a written test…

Listening

3 **2.21** You're going to listen to two friends, Chris and Jackie. First guess if 1–10 are true or false. Then listen to the first part of the conversation and check your answers to 1–4.

1 Jackie's determined to pass her driving test.
2 Chris has a driving license.
3 Chris thinks he took his first test too early.
4 In his first test, Chris parked illegally.
5 Chris had a different examiner in his second driving test.
6 Chris made a mistake at the beginning of his second test.
7 Chris was nervous throughout his second test.
8 Chris drove down a one-way street in the wrong direction.
9 Chris couldn't use the clutch properly.
10 The examiner refused to help Chris when he got into trouble.

4 **2.22** Before listening to the rest, do you want to change any of your answers 5–10? Listen to check.

5 Listen again. Order the Essential phrases 1–12 as you hear them.

6 Do you have equivalents for phrases 1–12 in your language? How often do you use them?

Tip
To comment or express surprise use *What* + noun, or *How* + adjective.
My two-year-old son gave me a flower yesterday.
What a lovely story. How sweet!

Grammar

7 Read the grammar box. Find one example of each rule in **2.22**.

Past modals

Form with modal verb + *have* + past participle.
1 Use *would have done* for hypothetical past actions.
2 Use *might / could have done* for a past hypothesis which is possibly true.
3 *Should have done* expresses regret or criticizes a past action.
4 Use *must have done* for a past hypothesis that you're certain is true.
5 Use *can't have done* to make a past hypothesis which you're certain didn't happen.

Remember?
Use *had to* to describe past obligation:
We had to pass an exam to go to secondary school.

Essential phrases for:

Building a story
☐ It gets worse.
☐ Did I ever tell you about it?
☐ What happened first was
☐ After that…

Responding to a story
[1] You didn't, did you? Wow!
☐ And what did he say?
☐ No way!
☐ Good for you.
☐ Right.
☐ You're joking!
☐ What went wrong?
☐ What a disaster!

28

Pronunciation

8 (2.23) In past modals, *have* is pronounced /əv/. This can make it very difficult to hear. Listen and circle the words you hear.

1 I *should put / have put* the bag in the boot.
2 She *must come / have come* on Saturday.
3 The teacher *might set / have set* different homework.
4 You *could run / have run* faster.
5 I *would quit / have quit* working for the company.

AB p. 91 Ex. 2 ▶

Reading

9 In pairs, Ⓐ read about disasters 1 and 2, Ⓑ read 3 and 4. Tell each other what you remember, then discuss the incidents. Hypothesise about what *must / might / could / should / can't* have happened.

Four sat-nav disasters

Some of the most spectacular disasters caused by satellite navigation systems - and how you can avoid having them happen to you.

1 Cars and water don't mix, as a driver in Glubczyce, Poland, found out. He kept following the instructions of his sat-nav – ignoring the road signs telling him that the road ahead was closed – and drove straight into the middle of a lake. Fortunately the man and his passengers got onto the roof of the car and were rescued by the emergency services.

2 Two robbers' criminal activities came to a sudden end when they were stopped by police in Doncaster, Yorkshire. They were found carrying thousands of euros and a number of stolen credit cards. But the strongest evidence was the sat-nav device, programmed with the addresses of all the Post Offices that they had robbed.

3 A hospital patient got taken on an eight-hour magical mystery tour, thanks to some London ambulance drivers. Completely trusting their sat-nav device, the ambulance crew took the patient to a hospital in Manchester, 200 miles away, when they were supposed to travel a mere 12 miles to Brentwood, Essex.

4 Redditch woman Paula Ceely escaped death en route to her boyfriend's house in Wales. Her sat-nav system took her to a large metal gate. Certain that this was the correct route, she opened the gate and, moments later, found herself in the path of a railway train. She jumped out of the way as the train smashed into her Renault Clio and carried it down the track. 'I'll never use a sat-nav again,' she told the Daily Telegraph.

Speaking

10 In pairs, get a card from your teacher. Take turns to tell your stories. Use the phrases on p. 28.

2 Revision

2A

1 Complete with adjectives from the snake. In pairs, decide if you both agree with them all.

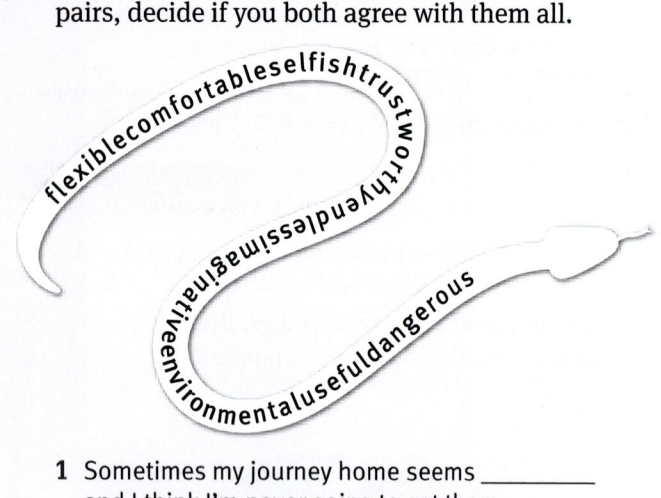

Snake words: flexible comfortable selfish trustworthy endless imaginative environmental useful dangerous

1 Sometimes my journey home seems _____ and I think I'm never going to get there.
2 My most _____ possession now is my mobile phone. I couldn't live without it.
3 I think I'm quite an _____ person. I'm always thinking of new ideas and I like art and drawing and things like that.
4 Riding a bike in the streets is really _____. There are so many accidents that you could have.
5 The biggest _____ problem in my country is pollution from industry.
6 Most people in my country are pretty _____. In general, I'd say they're very honest.
7 I never feel _____ meeting new people. I'm quite shy and I never know what to say.
8 I've never done yoga and to be honest, I don't think I'd enjoy it because I'm not very _____.
9 People today are much more _____ than in the past. They never want to share anything or help anyone else out.

2 Think of two more adjectives with the same suffixes as ex 1. Put them in a phrase.

3 Play DEFINE IT! Get some cards from your teacher.

4 Which prefix can be used with all these adjectives?

1 important, kind, likely, tidy — **un**
2 legal, legible, literate, logical — ___
3 mature, moral, patient, polite — ___
4 abled, honest, organised, satisfied — ___
5 accurate, correct, direct, edible — ___
6 regular, relevant, resistible, responsible — ___

2B

5 2.24 Listen to Chris speaking to his boss, Elena. Complete the notes.

1 Elena met Mary Peel at a sales conference in _____.
2 Mary has got _____ hair.
3 Chris went to _____ with Mary.
4 Elena and Chris' company make _____.
5 Mary works as a _____.
6 Chris is meeting Mary in their office at _____.

6 Listen again and count the question tags. Go to audio script 2.24 p. 108 to check.

7 Listen once more and mark the question tags U (up) or D (down) for intonation.

2C

8 In pairs, **A** read problem 1, **B** read problem 2. Explain the problem to your partner. Can you solve it? Get the answer from your teacher.

Problem 1

Last week Stefania's family were visiting her school. While her parents were speaking to the teachers, her cousin visited the library. In the library, her cousin went to look for a book and left an MP3 player on the desk. But then it was stolen! The head teacher, Mr Marlowe, investigated the theft.

Stefania's cousin <u>told</u> him that the library seemed to be empty. But the librarian informed Mr Marlowe that three boys had been there. The teacher asked the boys if they had stolen the MP3 player.

Nathan said he'd been working on the computer the whole time and that he hadn't stolen it. Julian said that he didn't know anything about the cousin and he'd never seen her. Carlos pointed out that he already had an MP4 player and asked why he would steal an MP3 player.

With this information, the head teacher knew who the thief was. Who was it?

Problem 2

Professor Martinez was recruiting new students for his university course in History. He was very impressed with an application from Jennifer Goode. However, one day his secretary mentioned that something was wrong with Jennifer's application. She explained that one of the emails looked like a fake.

Professor Jones, US expert in Mexican History:

"Jennifer is an excellent student who made very good progress over the three years that she was at our college."

Doctor Ruiz, a Spanish expert in the history of Madrid:

"Jennifer is extremely interested in all areas of world and European History."

Professor Mucklow, Britain's number one expert in Scottish history:

"Ms. Goode has consistently gotten the highest grades, especially now that she has specialized in Scottish history."

Professor Martinez realised that his secretary was right. He phoned the lecturer, who replied that this was not the first time someone had written a fake reference using his name. Which one was fake?

9 Underline eight reporting verbs in ex 8. (The first one has been done for you.) Rewrite the comments in direct speech.

10 In pairs, get a card from your teacher. Role-play the conversation.

11 Find six money idioms in the cards in ex 10. Which one do you use the most in your language?

12 In pairs, choose the correct option and answer the questions. Any coincidences?

   1 Did you forget *to do / doing* the homework for the class today?
   2 What do you enjoy *to do / doing* after your English lessons?
   3 Do you usually stop *to have / having* a coffee or a snack on your way to class?
   4 Do you mind *to speak / speaking* in front of the whole class?
   5 Did you remember *to bring / bringing* everything you need to class today?
   6 Do you want *to live / living* in an English-speaking country after your English course?

13 Do ex 3 in Word Bank 8 on p. 69.

Go to **Writing 2** p. 61 ▶

14 In pairs, ask and answer. Each ✱ = a missing word.

   1 ✱ ✱ know anybody who is ✱ a pension? ✱ they well-off or hard up?
   2 Should wealthy countries help ✱ ✱ are starving? What should they do?
   3 When ✱ the last time you were overcharged, e.g. in ✱ restaurant or hotel? ✱ you complain?
   4 Is it better to ✱ overdrawn or to ✱ a long-term loan from the bank?
   5 What kind ✱ people get ✱ grant? Wages? A salary?
   6 Why would you ✱ sickness or unemployment benefit?

15 In pairs, describe the cartoon. Use the future simple, future continuous and future perfect. Do you think this will really happen?

16 In pairs, close your books. Remember (and sketch) all you can from the picture.

17 Imagine you're a driving instructor, giving somebody their first lesson.

   A: Explain to B how to start, drive and stop the car.
   B: Explain to A how to turn left and how to park in a small space.

18 (2.25) Go to Word Bank 20, p. 75. Listen and chant the 8 dipthongs.

Song: *Baby you can drive my car* **by the Beatles**

To find the words, google *lyric* + the song title.

To find the video, google *video* + the song title and singer.

3A I am what I am

Grammar

1 In pairs, read an article about a successful advertising campaign. What was the message and why was it effective?

During the US presidential election campaign of 2008, a poster appeared on the New York Metro, in newspapers and other media. It had been designed by the advertising agency Grey to show the now president Barack Obama as a white male, and his white opponent John McCain as an African-American. It was the most successful advert of the campaign, and created a huge public debate.

2 Complete rules 1–6 with *a*, *the*, or Ø (= no article). Find an example of each rule in the article.

Articles (1)

1 Use _____ when there's only one, or when it's clear exactly which one it is.
2 Use _____ the first time something is mentioned.
3 Also use _____ to mean "one example of".
4 Use _____ for countable or uncountable nouns in general.
5 Use _____ + superlative adjectives.
6 Usually names of people and places use _____. However, a few places / names always need _____, e.g. newspapers, states.

Reading

3 In pairs, read the headline about Kate. Guess what the article will be about.

> I reckon it'll tell us about how she's…

RETOUCHING IS 'EXCESSIVE' SAYS SLIMLINE COVERGIRL KATE WINSLET

4 In pairs, cover the text and read it a line at a time. Can you guess what the first word on the next line will be? Count your correct guesses.

5 Who do you agree with, Kate or Dylan? Why?

A newly statuesque Kate Winslet stands on a pair of surprisingly thin legs on the cover of next month's GQ magazine. The result of a sudden diet? No, more like a little digital manipulation on the part of the magazine's art department.
The *Titanic* star, who has always made it clear that she doesn't believe a woman has to be slim to be attractive, has been criticised for being involved in the project. According to her agent, however, although the actress had approved the original photos, she was not asked about the digital changes.
In fact the star confirmed her attitude in the interview accompanying the photos. "Why is it that women think in order to be adored they have to be thin?" she says.
Meanwhile, the magazine's editor, Dylan Jones, while admitting that the photos had been doctored, claims that Kate has actually lost a lot of weight recently. "These pictures are not a million miles away from what she really looks like," he says. "Kate is currently thinner than I have ever seen her."
Ms Winslet herself, however, doesn't seem to share his opinion. "The retouching is excessive. I do not look like that and more importantly I don't desire to look like that," she said. "I actually have a Polaroid that the photographer gave me on the day of the shoot… I can tell you they've reduced the size of my legs by about a third. For my money it looks pretty good the way it was taken."

3A

Listening

6 🔊 3.1 Listen to part 1 of a conversation. How do Linus and Susannah know each other?

7 🔊 3.2 Listen to part 2 and look at the photo. How does Linus look different to this now / when he's at work?

8 In pairs, complete the table with as much as you can remember. Then listen again to check. Do you know anyone like Linus?

Name:	Linus Sutter		
From:		Hobbies:	
Father's Job:		Clothes at work:	
Mother's job:		Clothes in free time:	
Linus' job:		Current location:	

> **Remember?**
> The difference between *remind* and *remember*:
> You *remember* something. Something *reminds* you of the past.

Grammar

9 Match the highlighted phrases in audioscript 3.2 on p. 108 with rules 7–12.

> **Articles (2)**
> 7 For parts of someone's body, don't use *the*. Use *my*, *his*, *her*, etc.
> 8 Use *the* to talk about groups in society like *young*, *disabled*, *unemployed*.
> 9 To talk about a specific family, use *the* and make the surname plural.
> 10 To talk about something in general, use Ø. For specific examples, use *the*.
> 11 To describe your work, use *a* + profession.
> 12 Use *a* + a name to mean "one example of".

> **Tip**
> Use Ø for *school, hospital, prison* when you are a person inside the institution (a prisoner, nurse or student).
> *My dad's in hospital with a broken leg.*
> Use *the* when you work there, or when you're inside the building.
> *She works at the hospital.*

> AB p. 93 Ex. 4 ▶

Speaking

10 In pairs, imagine you've just met for the first time at a dinner party. Find out all you can about your partner. Include the information in ex 8. Try to use all 12 rules for Articles.

> *So, tell me a little about yourself. Why did your parents choose that name?*

UNIT 3   33

3B Man-flu

Speaking

1 **3.3 – 3.4** What do you do when you have a cold or the flu? Go to Word Bank 11, p. 70.

> *I go to bed with a hot drink as soon as I feel it coming, to stop it getting worse.*

2 **3.5** In pairs, listen and shadow-read the letter. How would you answer? Do men usually complain more than women?

Dear agonyaunt.com

Are all husbands like this?

It always starts the same way. He comes down to breakfast, tired and sighing, with a hand placed dramatically against his forehead. With slow, painful movements, he takes an aspirin and a glass of water before retreating noisily to the sofa. The central heating is put up to sub-tropical levels. But nothing seems to work. I know it's probably just a cold and he'll get over it in a couple of days, but he thinks he's dying. He says he's suffering like no one has ever suffered before, because, of course, when men get ill, they get ten times more ill than women, don't they? They suffer from 'Man-flu'. I know the doctors insist that there's no such thing, but try telling that to my patient sniffing and whimpering under the blankets. It's happening again today and I don't know what to do with him! Please advise…

Yours,
'wife-at-the-end-of-her-tether'

Pronunciation

3 **3.6** Listen and repeat. Notice the silent letters.

> aspirin   dramatically   medicine   suffered   temperature

4 **3.7** Cross out the silent letters in these words. Listen and check.

> comfortable   chocolate   different   evening
> every   family   interesting   separate   several   vegetable

In pairs, practise saying the words.

Listening

5 **3.8** Listen to four short conversations between Kevin and Fran. Answer the questions.

1 What symptoms does Kevin have?
2 Is Fran sympathetic in all of the conversations?
3 Which other people do they talk about?

Grammar

6 Order the words in green to complete these indirect questions. Go to **3.8** on p. 108 to check. What do you notice about word order?

a Would you like me *doctor make the appointment to an with*?
b Could you *cup make a tea of me*?
c Would you mind *my boss calling*?
d Do you know *if have house the any we in*?
e Do you mind *some the to get going chemist's to*?
f I was wondering whether *should you go the doctor's to*.

Look again at a–f in ex 6. Circle the rules 1–4.

Indirect questions

Use indirect questions to offer or request help. They're longer and more formal than direct Q's.

1 *Would you like* is followed by *–ing / the infinitive*.
2 Use *do* and *will / would + mind*.
3 Word order is the *same as / different to* direct questions.
4 Most indirect questions end with + ❓ except for those beginning with *Would you like / I was wondering…*

> AB p. 94 Ex. 5 ▶

Tip

Do / Would you mind? means *Is it a problem?*. People can answer both 'no' or 'yes' meaning 'it's no problem'.
Do you mind if I use your phone?
No, no, go ahead. / Yes, of course.

Reading

7 In pairs, Ⓐ quickly read paragraph 1 of the article. Ⓑ read paragraph 2. Share what you remember. Do you think the article will be scientific / informative, academic or funny?

8 In pairs do the same with paragraphs 3 and 4, then 5 and 6. Then match sentences a–f to gaps 1–6.

a They seek conflict where women try to create harmony.
b The situation isn't helped by the male enthusiasm for red meat and fried food.
c What's more important: watching the football or cleaning the bathroom floor?
d Men, by contrast, often avoid seeking professional medical advice until the last minute, which is not to be advised.
e Surely, we're not just victims of biology, forced to play out a script that has already been written?
f Men have more of the former and women more of the latter.

9 Do you agree with the comments in bold?

Warning! Being a man can damage your health

Is it really true that **women can't read maps?** (1) _____ How is it that **women can chat for hours**, while men never listen to a word they say? When it comes to the differences between men and women, it is impossible to tell where truth ends and stereotyping begins. However, there is one difference that is certainly true. Across the world, in all societies and at all income levels, women live longer than men. Why? Can it be true that being a man is bad for you?

One big difference between men and women comes from the hormones testosterone and oestrogen. (2) _____ Testosterone is the hormone that makes men look the way they are. It creates body hair and muscle. It also causes baldness, but a little hair loss seems small punishment for a stronger, faster body. Except for one other thing. Testosterone does strange things to men's minds.

It is now believed that testosterone makes men take risks. It is no accident that men enjoy physical, extreme sports. **Men are also more likely to be involved in violent behaviour** . (3) _____ All this means that men find themselves in dangerous situations much more than women, and they are more likely to die in accidents, for example, than women are.

On the other hand, having higher oestrogen levels is definitely an advantage for women. Oestrogen has many positive effects, but one in particular is that it protects the heart. So women are much less likely to suffer from heart disease.

But can we really blame nature for everything? (4) _____ There are, after all, many men who do live to a ripe old age, and live healthy independent lives into their nineties. How have they managed to live so well?

There are other things happening here. If men do live shorter lives than women, it could be that lifestyle is a

factor. **Men are much more likely to live unhealthily:** drinking alcohol and smoking are two male habits that can shorten life expectancy. (5) _____

By contrast, **women tend to take care of themselves better**. They are much more aware of health and illness, and are used to regular visits to the doctor. (6) _____

All this evidence suggests that the traditional idea of women as the weaker sex is outdated. **Being a man is much more dangerous.** So when your father, brother or son is suffering from a nasty bout of man-flu, remember to give him all the care he needs. Sometimes, it's hard to be a man!

Speaking

10 In threes, find out who's the healthiest. Ⓐ and Ⓑ ask Ⓒ. Use this checklist. Include at least two indirect questions. Then swap roles.

How healthy is your lifestyle?

1 Do you have a healthy diet? Five portions of fruit and veg a day? A lot of fatty food or red meat?
2 Do you have any unhealthy habits? Too much caffeine, too little water, etc.?
3 How much exercise do you do? Half an hour, five times a week? Usually walk, ride a bike, or drive?
4 Do you live in a noisy area? Enough space? Somewhere quiet?
5 Are you generally calm? Do you get angry easily? Often get stressed?

Essential phrases

I'm not really bothered about…

… isn't really a problem for me.

I know you're supposed to… but I don't because…

Usually I… but occasionally I…

I try to…

I probably… too much / often / little

3C The art of the street

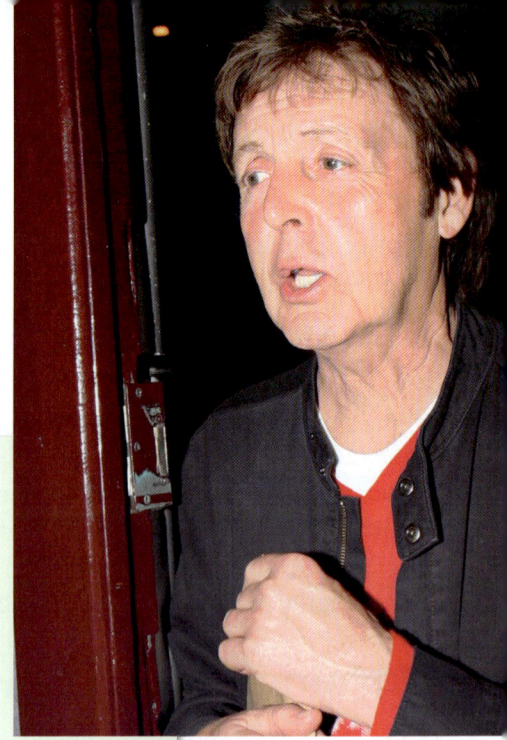

Speaking

1 In 30 seconds, read the story. In pairs, remember all the details you can. What's your usual reaction to buskers? Have you ever met or seen a famous person? Who would you most like to see busking?

I don't usually give them any money, unless they're really good.

> Many of the world's most famous artists started their careers as buskers: street musicians playing for a few coins in public. But very few of them have gone back to the streets after achieving world-wide fame. But one day, Paul McCartney, the ex-Beatle, did just that.
>
> "It was for a film thing and it was something I'd always wanted to do. So I scruffed myself up a bit, put on a false beard and shades, and went down to Leicester Square tube station. It was really cool."
>
> "A couple of people came up and said, 'Is it you?' but I just said, 'Oh, no.'
>
> "But I got a few shillings and I thought, 'This doesn't feel right'. So I gave it to charity."

shilling: an old British coin, worth a small amount of money.

Remember...
... the difference between *few*, *a few*, *a couple of* and *a small amount*?

2 **3.9 – 3.10** When was the last time you complained to someone about something? Go to Word Bank 12 p. 71.

Listening

3 **3.11** Listen to two friends, Helen and Piet. Write T (true) or F (false).

1 The busker's playing jazz music. ___
2 The busker's been playing for quite a long time. ___
3 The volume of the music is a problem for Helen and Piet. ___
4 Almost everybody hates the music that he is playing. ___
5 Helen has complained to the police about him. ___
6 Piet decides to speak to the busker about the music. ___

Grammar

4 **3.11** Circle the correct verb form. Listen again to check.

1 ☐ That violinist *has been driving / has driven me* mad!
2 ☐ He's *played / been playing* all day long.
3 ☐ He's *played / been playing* that song about five times already!
4 ☐ People *have given / have been giving* him loads of money.
5 ☐ The police *have spoken / have been speaking* to him already.
6 ☐ She's *lived / She's been living here* all her life

5 Match the sentences in ex 4 with rules a–f. Some rules match with more than one sentence.

Present Perfect Continuous	Present Perfect Simple
a To describe an action which may or may not be finished *I've been washing up.*	b Use for an action which is finished. *I've done the washing up.*
c To say how long an action lasted *I've been working on the computer for hours.*	d Use to describe the amount of things that you have completed *I've written about twenty emails.*
e For more temporary situations. *I've been living here for a month.*	f Use for situations that are more permanent. *I've worked here for twenty years.*

AB p. 95 Ex. 4 ▶

Tip
Don't use continuous tenses with non-action verbs (*know*, *like*, *believe*, etc).
I've never known anything like it!

6 In pairs. Get a card from your teacher.

36

Reading

7 Quickly read paragraph 1 of the article. When was the last time you saw a living statue? Describe it.

8 In pairs, **A** read paragraphs 2–3. **B** read paragraphs 4–5. Describe two living statues in your half of the text. Which one is the most interesting?

9 Read paragraph 6. How did Jankowski make art imitate life? Do you prefer living statues or traditional ones? Would you like to have a statue made of you?

Life imitates art

1   Barcelona has always been a city where art is everywhere, and nowhere more so than on its most famous street, the Ramblas. Beneath the statue of Christopher Columbus, artists sell paintings and drawings of the city and tourists laugh while cartoonists draw their friends. Go further up the street however, and you will find artists as original as any of the installations in the city's modern art galleries – and a lot more fun. For the Ramblas is home to Barcelona's living statues.

2   The Brazilian footballer Ronaldinho (or perhaps a lookalike?) practises his tricks; and Julius Caesar himself surveys the crowds. Many of these artists have been working the street for three or four years or more. They are now as much a part of the city's history as the great painter Picasso, who grew up in the Catalan capital.

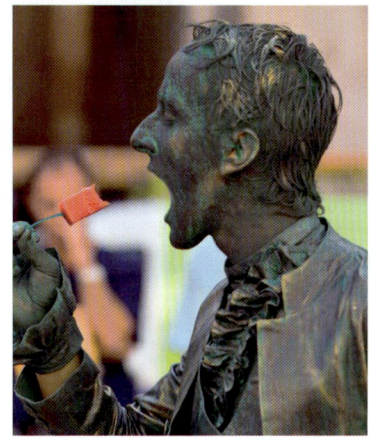

3   The statues do nothing until a coin drops in a can or hat. Then, suddenly, dramatically, figures that haven't been moving for hours, jump into life. Dancers dance and cyclists dressed as skeletons start pedalling furiously round.

4   One warning: after the living statues have been waiting for hours at a time, they are quick to complain if people steal a photo without paying. Not all of the statues can move to show their anger, however. One of the strangest is a man whose head sticks out of a plate of spaghetti, with his body hidden beneath a restaurant table.

5   Interestingly, often these street entertainers are as much foreigners as the tourists who pay them. One example is the Argentinean who is always on the street as his famous compatriot, the revolutionary Che Guevara, complete with uniform and gun.

6   And in a strange case of art imitating life, "Che" was one of the statues chosen by German sculptor Christian Jankowski to be turned into a real statue. Jankowski was inspired to immortalise three of the street performers in bronze. He then placed his sculptures on the Ramblas, where people have been examining them with confusion, suddenly unsure as to which of the statues were real, and which are just people in disguise!

Speaking

10 Role-play in pairs. **A** you're the living statue. **B** you're the busker. Tell your partner what you've been doing today.

Essential phrases

Today, I've mostly been…
I'm exhausted because…
I've done good business today…
It's been a tough / easy day for me because…

3D Changing times

Speaking

1 (3.12) – (3.13) In pairs, describe the people in the photos. Do you like their 'look'? Guess which decade these photos were taken in. Go to Word Bank 13, p. 71

I think this one must have been taken during the last decade. It looks very recent.

A

B

C

Listening

2 (3.14) Listen to three conversations about photos A–C. Do the speakers like or dislike the photos?

1 Dan ☺ ☹ Lucy ☺ ☹
2 Chris ☺ ☹ Julie ☺ ☹
3 Tim ☺ ☹ Chizuko ☺ ☹

3 Which of the six people can you identify in the photos? Listen again and check. Do you have any similarly embarrassing photos of your own?

My passport photo makes me look about 50!

Tip
Unstressed words are often difficult to hear. Try to listen for the stressed words (said more slowly and loudly), which carry the main meaning.

Grammar

4 Look at the yellow sentences in (3.14) on p. 109. What tenses are they? Do they refer to the past or the present?

5 Match the sentence halves for rules 1 and 2.

wish and if only

Use *wish* and *if only*

| 1 + Past Simple | a for regrets about the past. |
| 2 + Past Perfect | b for disappointment with the present. |

If only is slightly stronger than *wish*.

AB p. 96 Ex. 5 ▶

Remember?
Use *wish* / *if only* with past modals *would* and *could*, NOT *will* and *can*.
I wish people would wear clothes like that now.
If only I had their email addresses.

Pronunciation

6 In pairs, look at (3.15) on p. 109. Guess which words in each sentence will be said most slowly and with the strongest stress?

7 (3.15) Listen and check. Underline the two most stressed words. Then practise saying them in pairs.

8 Do you have any wishes or regrets?

I wish I'd never had a tattoo.

Reading

9 Read the two letters to a problem page. Think of three pieces of advice you'd give each of them if you were Samantha.

Dear Samantha

I really wish I looked like I did twenty years ago. The thing is that I'm getting grey hair and wrinkles and I'm starting to feel a bit old. Do you have any advice for a guy like me?

Fading fast!

Dear Samantha

I've had the same look for the last five years and I'm getting a bit bored of it. But I don't have a lot of money. If only I knew how to change my look without it costing the earth, I'd make the change tomorrow! Any ideas?

Dull Dora

10 In pairs, read and match Samantha's answers, a–f, to *Fading* or *Dora*. How much of her advice is the same as yours? Then choose the best suggestion for each person.

a You could always dye it, but that doesn't always work. For example, black eyelashes don't really go with blonde hair. Or, if you're feeling really adventurous, shave it all off. A friend of mine did that last year and he looked ten years younger. He told me he wished he'd done it years ago.

b Make up is always a quick fix. The eyes are a really important part of the face and it's amazing what a difference a bit of mascara can make. Apply the make-up gently to your eyelashes and soon you'll be feeling different, mysterious, and exotic!

c It's not necessary to spend a lot of money at the hairdressers. One thing you can do is simply move your parting from one side of your face to the other. Suddenly, everybody will be wondering what's different about you! Alternatively, swap your parting for a fringe or vice-versa.

d Don't make the mistake of thinking that shaving damages your face. In fact it smooths the skin and is one reason why men often have fewer lines than women when they reach old age. So forget designer stubble, and get the razor out every day.

e How about coloured contact lenses?
I started wearing them at dinner parties myself last year, and everyone was wondering what was different about me. I wish I'd thought of it years ago!

f It's amazing what an effect your hands can have on your age. If you don't want to have a manicure, you can always use special creams and moisturisers at home that will soon have your fingers and nails looking shiny and young again.

Speaking

11 In pairs. Get a card from your teacher. Look at the pictures and imagine what the people are saying. Then role play one of the situations.

3E Gadget mania!

Speaking

1. **3.16 – 3.17** In fours, describe all the inventions on this page in as much detail as you can. Guess what they're used for. Go to Word Bank 14, p. 72.

   It looks like a cone.

Remember?
3 phrases for describing objects:
It's used for –*ing*. It looks like…
It might be…
It looks like an ice-cream cone.

Reading

2. In fours, in 40 seconds, each read about one invention, A–D. Report back all you can remember to your group. How many gadgets did you guess correctly?

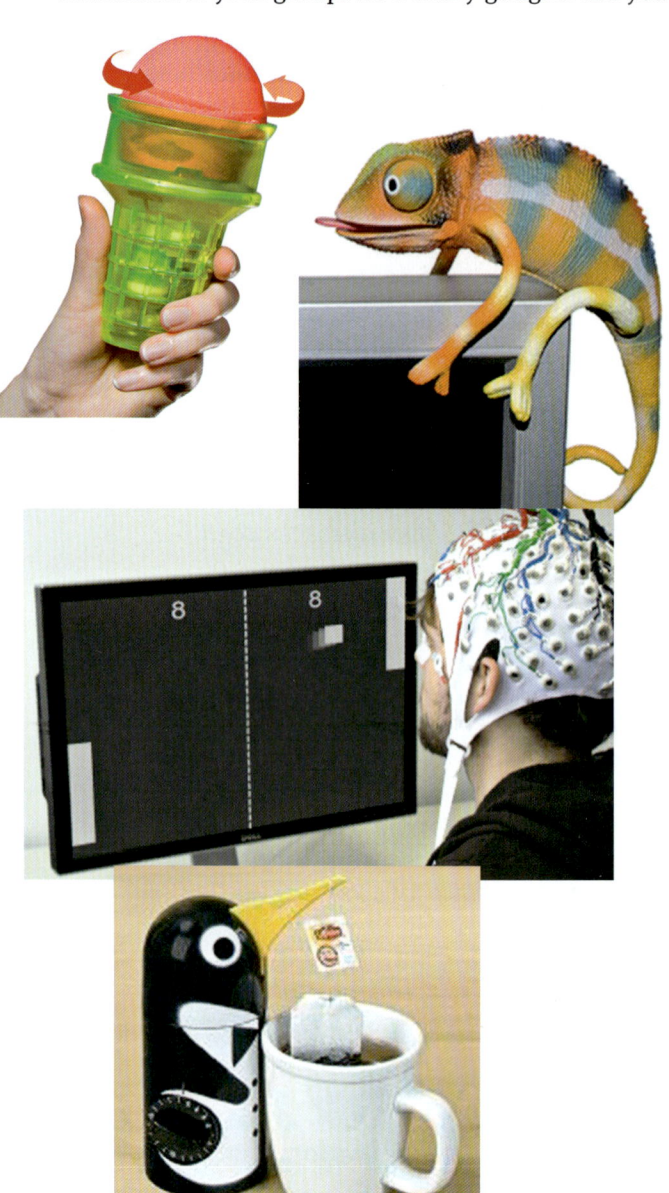

A This looks exactly like an everyday ice-cream cone. However, what's special about this particular invention is that it actually moves. It's used by people who want to turn their ice cream around but don't want to move their hand at the same time. This **handy** gadget is made of plastic and is available in red, green and orange.

B This essential item is the USB chameleon. He's made of latex and his tail is extremely useful for attaching to a mug or a pc monitor. If you connect him to the USB port on your computer, he moves his eyes and shows you his tongue. But be warned: although he'll cost you €15 a time, he doesn't change colour, unlike his reptilian **namesake**.

C No, this isn't the latest Wii sensation enabling you to play water polo from your sofa. This is the Berlin Brain-Computer Interface, invented at Germany's Fraunhofer Institute. This **cutting-edge** technology uses a cap made of leather and wires. By reading the subject's brain, this device enables users to select letters on a screen. In effect, it's a telepathic typewriter!

D Here we have the penguin tea timer. Attach a tea bag to his **beak**, and dip it into a cup of hot water. You set the clock by his side, and then, when it is finished, he lifts the tea bag out and makes a little noise to tell you that your drink is ready. Who needs a watch?

3. Quickly read all the texts. What do you think the words in **bold** mean?

4. Answer these questions.
   1. Which of these devices are only decorative?
   2. Who would benefit from the Berlin Brain-Computer Interface?
   3. How many different materials are the inventions made of?
   4. Are any of these inventions toys or games?

Tip
Use *made from* when the original substance has been changed, and *made of* when it has not.
Paper's made from wood.
This table's made of wood.

Listening

5 **3.18** Listen to conversations 1–3 about gadgets. In pairs, after each one, say what you think the gadgets are.

6 **3.18** In pairs. Which conversation did these sentences come from? Why? Listen and check.

   a These things are designed to be used by people like you.
   b You just can't leave work behind, can you?
   c Oh, this is heavy!

Pronunciation

7 **3.19** Listen again to these sentences. How are the people feeling?

   1 Will you put that thing away!
   2 We're supposed to be on holiday!
   3 This? Ah! This is my new toy.
   4 But we don't need things like this!
   5 Dad! I've told you how to do this a million times.
   6 What's that supposed to mean?

8 Underline the words in ex 7 that the speakers stress for emphasis (to show anger or excitement). Then listen again to check your answers. In pairs, practise saying the sentences quickly.

Grammar

9 Order the green words in these sentences.

   a If you'd on an computer wouldn't be out-of-office your you message put getting all these emails anyway!
   b If I have had hadn't it I got today wouldn't it so cheaply.
   c If you that it hadn't button would have started pressed automatically.

10 Circle the correct rules. Do you use similar tenses for the third conditional in your language?

   Third conditional

   If + *Past Perfect / Present Perfect*, + would + have been

   Use the third conditional to describe *real / hypothetical* situations *in the future / past*.

   AB p. 97 Ex. 5 ▶

Speaking

11 In pairs, quickly complete these sentences. Race the other students in the class. Then find another pair with a similar answer to you, and ask for more details.

   If my parents hadn't met…

   If I'd never met my boyfriend/ girlfriend/best friend…

   If I'd stayed in bed this morning…

   I wouldn't have joined the class if…

   If I'd had more brothers or sisters…

   I wouldn't have left my last job if…

   If I'd gone shopping yesterday…

   If I'd/hadn't gone out last night…

UNIT 3 41

3F Artist at work!

Speaking

1 (3.20) In pairs, guess who painted these pictures. Which one do you prefer? Describe the differences between them. Go to Word Bank 15, p. 72.

Speaking

2 Play EIGHT DIFFERENCES. Get a card from your teacher.

> **Remember?**
> Uses of *on*:
> *a picture **on** the wall / the cover* (= touching the surface)
> ***on** TV / CD / the Internet / the radio / a memory stick* (= electronic medium)

Listening

3 (3.21) In pairs, guess if facts 1–6 are true or false. Listen to the first part of the podcast about the artist's life to check.

1. Congo died recently.
2. He only made two or three paintings in his lifetime.
3. His paintings sell for a lot of money.
4. He's never had an exhibition of his paintings.
5. He was a celebrity pet.
6. Congo only painted.
7. Many famous artists like his work.

4 (3.22) In pairs, do you want to change any of your answers now? Listen to part 2 of the podcast and check.

Grammar

5 Match the words in the box with their past simple/past participles in audioscript (3.21) and (3.22) on p. 109.

> beat   choose   draw   feed   hang   seek   spread   teach

6 Complete the table with the verb forms from ex 5.

> **Irregular verbs**
>
> English has over 150 irregular verbs. As you come across new ones, try to match them to spelling and pronunciation patterns of other irregular verbs you know.
>
> Similar forms as
> 1. bet, bet, bet — *beat* _____
> 2. buy, bought, bought — *teach* _____
> 3. know, knew, known — _____
> 4. read, read, read — _____
> 5. sting, stung, stung — _____
> 6. freeze, froze, frozen — _____

7 Think of four more irregular verbs that you could add to 1–6 in the grammar box.

> AB p. 98 Ex. 2 ▶

> **Tip**
> Some verbs have both a regular (*-ed*) and an irregular form (*-t*) like *burn*, *dream*, *learn* and *spell*. In American English, the *-t* forms are not widely used, except for *burnt*.
> *There are several animals who have learnt to paint.*

Speaking

8 In pairs, play ABOUT ME. Toss a coin. Heads = move one square. Tails = move two squares. Answer the question (your partner should ask at least one follow-up question). The first player to finish is the winner.

About Me

1 START ➡	**2** What pictures are hanging in your house?	**3** What was the last interesting website you found on the Internet?	**4** When did you last spend a lot of money in one day?
8 When was the last time that you swam in the sea / a river?	**7** What is the strangest thing that you've ever eaten?	**6** Move forward two spaces	**5** When was the last time that you bought a present for someone?
9 Name three English words that mean something different in your language.	**10** What's the best photograph that you have ever taken?	**11** Have you ever ridden a horse, a motorbike or a skateboard? When? Where?	**12** Miss a turn
16 Move forward one spaces	**15** Describe a new song that you heard recently and that you liked.	**14** What do you put in your pockets / bag when you leave the house?	**13** Have you ever seen a rare animal or endangered species? Where?
17 How many texts and emails do you send a day?	**18** What were you wearing yesterday?	**19** Who is the oldest person you know?	**20** FINISH!

9 <u>Underline</u> the irregular verb in each square of the game. Do you know its infinitive, past simple and past participle form? Check your answers on page 76.

UNIT 3   43

3 Revision

3A 1 In pairs, complete the squares with *the*, *a / an*, *your* or Ø (no article). Then play the game. **A** toss a coin. (Heads = move one square. Tails = move two squares.) Talk about the topic on the square for a minute. **B** listen and ask two follow-up questions. Then **B** toss a coin and take your turn.

Change squares with Student B!	Do you have _____⁵ rich aunt or _____⁶ unusual uncle? Are you close to them?	What was _____⁷ most useful subject you studied at _____⁸ school? Why? And _____⁹ least?
Can you remember all the words in Word Bank 11 (illnesses)?		*Miss a turn!*
Have you ever broken _____⁴ limb? How? Is it 100% back to _____³ normal now?		Do you have _____¹⁰ pet? Whose decision was it to get it? Are you into _____¹¹ animals?
Go forward one square		**FINISH! YOU WIN!**
What's _____² most beautiful place you know? How many times have you been?		
Describe _____¹ dish you make well. How did you learn? How often do you make it?	**START A ← B →**	What were _____¹² last two films you saw at _____¹³ cinema? What were they like?
		Who's _____¹⁴ most famous living person from your country? Are you _____¹⁵ fan?
FINISH! YOU WIN!		*Go forward two squares*
Are you into _____²⁴ sports? Watching or playing? Which one(s)? Do you prefer _____²⁵ other hobbies?		Do you live in _____¹⁶ rented house or _____¹⁷ own flat? Describe _____¹⁸ room you like best in it.
Which countries share _____²² border with _____²³ yours? Have you visited any of them?		Can you remember all the words in Word Bank 10 (cars and driving)?
Answer one of Student A's squares.	Describe _____¹⁹ route home from _____²⁰ school. Do you get _____²¹ public transport?	*Miss a turn!*

3B 2 (3.23) Look at p. 70. Find words that rhyme with these. Listen and check. Do any of the rhymes or spellings surprise you?

> believer   do   law
> literature   note   off   please
> rolled   vacant   worse

Believer rhymes with fever.

3 (3.24) In pairs, read five folk cures. Do you believe they all work? Listen and check.

Before people had modern medicines, they used 'folk cures': ideas that a plant, a herb, or even changing your behaviour could cure a disease. Lots of them are nonsense, but perhaps others really work. Here are five folk cures – do you think they work?

Chocolate can cure a cough.

Eating bananas can prevent dry eyes.

If you have a sore throat, drink honey and lemon in hot water.

If you burn yourself, put butter on the injury.

Ginger is a natural remedy for flu.

4 Do you know any other 'folk cures' like this? In fours, share and compare ideas. Then tell the class your most credible one. Whose idea is 'the best'?

> *My grandma swore by this idea for curing flu. She said...*

44

5 In pairs, think of a synonym for the words in Word bank 12 on p. 71. Do they work with the same preposition?

6 Play WHAT HAVE THEY BEEN UP TO? Get a card from your teacher.

7 Choose the correct option. Then listen and take turns to tell the joke. Who can tell it best?

Three men were stuck on a desert island after their boat had sunk in the Pacific. Then, one day they found a magic lamp. They rubbed the lamp and a genie appeared. The genie offered them three wishes. The first man said "I wish I ¹*never got / had never got* on that boat." The genie nodded and the man disappeared. The second man said "I wish I ²*was sitting / am sitting* in my living room back home – far away from here." The genie smiled and the man disappeared. Then he asked the third man, "what is your wish?" And the man said "I don't know. I can't decide. I wish the other two ³*are / were* here to help me choose…"

And 'kazam'! In a flash, the genie disappeared and the other two were both back on the desert island again, looking completely shocked. Their shock quickly turned to extreme anger.

"Er… sorry!" said the third man. "I wish I ⁴*didn't say / hadn't said* that now."

8 In pairs, if a genie suddenly appeared and offered you three wishes, what would you choose?

I'd choose to be able to fly.

Go to **Writing 3** p. 62 ▶

9 In pairs, take turns to explain to an English-speaking Martian, the difference between:
- a piercing and pierced ears
- contact lenses and glasses?
- an eyelash and an eyebrow?
- a beard and stubble?
- a parting and a fringe?
- grey hair and dyed hair?
- a wig and a moustache?

Well, a piercing is a piece of metal that you put anywhere in your skin. Pierced ears are ears with holes pierced in them.

10 Do ex 4 on page 71.

11 Play TWENTY QUESTIONS in threes. Get a card from your teacher.

12 On a piece of paper, complete this sentence:
If I hadn't come to school today, I…
Give it to your teacher who reads out the sentences. Guess who wrote them.

13 Play IRREGULAR RACE. In pairs, write down all the irregular verbs you know beginning with these letters? Ⓐ use group 1, Ⓑ group 2. You have only two minutes!

| Group 1 | B | F | L | S | W |
| Group 2 | C | D | H | R | T |

14 Circle the odd one out. Why is it different?

1	crew	police	society	team
2	coin	expenses	fee	jewellery
3	beak	forehead	nails	skin
4	hazardous	hilarious	nasty	scary
5	average	fraction	percentage	portion
6	dishwasher	gimmick	kettle	monitor
7	attractive	convenient	excessive	handy

15 🔊 3.25 Go to Word Bank 20, p. 75. Listen and chant the 9 unvoiced consonants.

Song: *Paint it Black* by The Rolling Stones

To find the words, google *lyric* + the song title.

To find the video, google *video* + the song title and singer.

UNIT 3 **45**

4A Live: tonight!

Speaking

1 **4.1 – 4.2** In threes, do the web survey. Then go to Word Bank 16, p. 73.

> The new Coldplay album is my all time favourite.

Remember?
Questions often end with a preposition.
What are you talking about?

We at Live: tonight magazine want to know about your 'faves'. Please take a minute to answer our survey.

What album/song have you most listened to?
Which bands have you seen live most often?
What's the best gig you've ever been to?
Which is your favourite live music venue?

Reading

2 In pairs, **A** read text 1, **B** read text 2, then close your books. Tell your partner everything you remember about your festival. Open your books and read the other text. Did your partner remember everything?

3 Have you been to either of these festivals? Which would you like to go to? Why?

1 Bregenz Festival, Austria

Rising from the calm waters of Lake Constance, a giant skeleton smiles as it turns the pages of an enormous book. Below, tiny performers come and go in a performance of Verdi's opera *A Masked Ball*. This was the setting of the 2000 opera festival held in Bregenz.

The Bregenz Festival has been producing extraordinary shows like this for over sixty years. As the highlight of the festival, which takes place in July and August, there is a production of a major opera on the Floating Stage. In 2008, the stage was filled with by a giant eye for Puccini's *Tosca*. If you missed that performance, don't worry. You can still see it in the James Bond movie *Quantum of Solace*.

For those with theatrical tastes, there is more than just opera on the menu. From 2007, drama has also appeared on the festival programme, with plays being shown in various venues throughout the town.

2 Festival Au Desert, Mali

On a cold January morning in Essakane, mysterious songs rise over the desert. The wind is already blowing and the sand gets everywhere: in your hair, in your skin and in your clothes. All around, there is the noise of camels. This is how the day begins at the Festival Au Desert, one of the world's most exotic music events.

Essakane itself lies in the heart of the Sahara desert, a further two-hour journey from Timbuktu. It is so distant and hard to reach that even the festival organisers advise that 'it can be difficult and potentially hazardous travelling alone' to the event. Nevertheless, many visitors do arrive to enjoy three days of music and dance, headlined by some of the world's most famous bands.

At the heart of the proceedings is African music. Fans can get close to some of the best performers on the continent, singing right next to them, as though they were simple travelling musicians, and not artists who are famous all over the world.

Listening

4 (4.3) Listen to *Phil*, *Stefi* and *Judy* describe the first gig they ever went to. Complete the chart.

	Phil	Stefi	Judy
Who / see?			
Who / go with?			
Any good? Why (not)?			

Tip

In formal situations, use *be* + infinitive to talk about future plans.
The new art gallery is to open in February.

Be about to is less formal and more common:
I'm about to eat, I'll call you back in a minute.

Grammar

5 Match the rules to the yellow examples in audioscript (4.3) on p. 109.

The future in the past

In stories, we often talk about the future in the past. Use the same rules as for reported speech.

am / is / are going to → was / were going to
He was going to come to lunch but he's changed his mind.
will / won't → would / wouldn't
He said he wouldn't be coming to stay with us in the summer.
am / is / are to → was / were to
The meeting was to start at 7 pm
Present Continuous → Past Continuous
They were leaving later in the afternoon.

AB p. 100 Ex. 3 ▶

Pronunciation

6 (4.4) Listen again to sentences 1 to 6. Draw an arrow at the end of the sentence to show if the intonation rises or falls.

1 So we went along to the venue and we saw this amazing gig.
2 And he died the next day, I think. 27. A tragic loss.
3 It was a complete disaster.
4 I went with my friends to see Coldplay last year! They were great!
5 And Coldplay! It was so cool.
6 There was one scary moment though…

7 Circle the rule. In pairs, practise saying the sentences in ex 6.

Use *falling / rising* intonation to give good news and *falling / rising* for bad news.

Speaking

8 In groups, have you ever been to a big rock festival? Who was on? Did you stay overnight? Was it as good as you'd hoped?

> *Only once. I went to Rock in Rio a few years ago.*

9 In pairs, imagine you've seen three bands at a festival. Share your experiences with another pair.

Essential phrases

We were planning to… but…
All in all…
The best thing was…
There were a few problems…
We stayed in…
The weather was…
One surprise was…

4B How technology can change your life

Speaking

1 In groups, read four opinions on technology from a web forum. Do you agree or disagree?

> "When I left school, we didn't have the Internet and so I lost touch with a lot of my friends. But at least I managed to keep in touch with my good friends, and they're real people, not just a list of a names on a website. We have a reunion every year in the fall."
> — Hitomi, 48, Osaka

> "Nowadays, everything has to be modern or people aren't interested. Old movies? Forget it! And old means anything that isn't in high definition and produced after 2001!"
> — Maria, 41, Paraguay.

> "Kids these days spend all their time playing on the computer and never go outside. It's made them lazy. They don't go out, don't walk anywhere, take the elevator instead of the stairs. It's terrible."
> — Lola, 57, Turin.

> "What would I do without the Internet? I get ideas from it all the time. Like, if I want to bake some cookies or I've only got only eggplant and zucchini in the fridge, I go online and find a recipe in seconds.
> — Curtis, 37, St, Louis.

I know what she means but I just don't agree.

2 (4.5) Find six American English words in the forum. Go to Word bank 17, p. 73.

> **Tip**
> Use *be / keep in / lose touch* to mean you're speaking or communicating with someone.
> *I'm still in touch with all my friends from school.*

Listening

3 In pairs, look at the photos. What are the people doing? Have you ever done anything like this?

4 (4.6) Listen to two friends, Jong-Kyu and Hannah, talking about a computer game. Are 1–5 true, false or not given?

1. Jong-Kyu's been playing musical instruments for a long time.
2. He only had one game when he got his games system.
3. He's one of the best Guitar Hero players in the world.
4. The other people in his band live in another country.
5. Hannah also spends a lot of time in front of the computer.

5 (4.7) In pairs, listen to a doctor and a patient. Ⓐ make notes about what the doctor says. Ⓑ Do the same for the patient. What can you remember? Listen again to check.

Grammar

6 Look at the yellow phrases in (4.6) and (4.7) on p. 109 and match the sentence halves 1–5.

Quantifiers

Use quantifiers like *much, many, little* to say whether there's a large or small amount of a noun.

1	*Plenty of, loads of* and *a large number of* mean	almost none
2	*A bit of* and *a few* mean	an imprecise number (not large but more than two)
3	*Several* means	some (probably not a large amount) — 2
4	*Hardly any* means	a small amount of
5	*A little* means	lots of

7 Which phrases in the Grammar box can you use with:

a C nouns? b U nouns? c both C and U nouns?

8 In pairs, compare how much / little you have of these things? Talk about them using quantifiers.

> *I've got very little free time just now as I'm teaching in 3 schools.*

friends from other countries
things to do today
free time in the evenings
money on you
pronunciation problems in English
stress in your life

AB p. 101 Ex. 2 ▶

Reading

9 In pairs, read the news story and complete 1–6.

1 When Patrick saw her, Camille...
2 He didn't speak to her at first because...
3 The response to his website was...
4 He eventually heard from...
5 Camille's reaction was...
6 After they finally spoke, he...

10 (4.8) In pairs, guess how the story ended. Listen and check. Were you right? Do you know any similar love stories?

Love at first sight

It happens to us all. You're walking down the sidewalk or waiting in line at the drug store, when, suddenly, you see the person of your dreams. Perhaps it's the way they move or the color of their hair. But do you go and talk to them? Well, here's the story of one young New Yorker in just that dilemma.

For Web designer Patrick Moberg, 21, from Brooklyn, it was love at first sight when he locked eyes with a woman while riding the subway in Manhattan one evening. She was writing in her journal.

The shy romantic, who moved to the Big Apple from Nashville, was building up the courage to speak to her, but the train was so full that he lost her in the crowd when they both got off. So he set up a website dedicated to finding the mystery woman – www.nygirlofmydreams.com.

He drew a picture of the girl and posted his cell phone number, e-mail address and a request for help finding her. It worked.

Within hours Moberg's inbox was full and his phone was ringing non-stop.

Amazingly in a city of 8 million people, a friend of the mystery woman contacted him and sent him a picture so he could confirm her friend's identity. "Found Her! Seriously!" the notice on his website said.

"We've been put in touch with one another and we'll see what happens."

The mysterious subway brunette was named as Camille Hayton, an intern at magazine BlackBook from Melbourne, Australia, who also lives in Brooklyn. "This is crazy. I can't believe it's happening." Hayton, 22, told the New York Post.

But Moberg said he will do no more interviews. "In our best interest, there will be no more updates to this website," he wrote. "Unlike all the romantic comedies and bad pop songs, you'll have to make up your own ending for this."

Speaking

11 In threes, play BACK TOGETHER. Get a card from your teacher.

Remember?

Spelling differences between UK and US English (UK first):
colour / color, litre / liter, catalogue / catalog, realise / realize.

UNIT 4   49

4C Any volunteers?

Speaking

1 **4.9 – 4.10** What are volunteers A–C doing? Which would you prefer to do? Word Bank 18, p. 74.

I've worked as a volunteer but nothing like this. I was a security guard at...

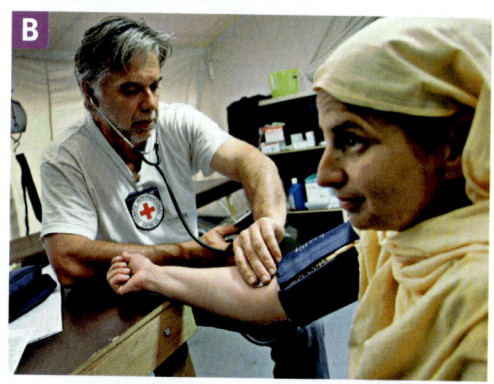

Reading

2 **4.11** Listen and shadow read paragraph 1 of the article. Is there any hope for the cheetah? Any pronunciation surprises?

3 **Ⓐ** read paragraph 2. **Ⓑ** read paragraph 3. **Ⓐ** explain the work of the CCB. **Ⓑ** explain why the cheetah population doesn't grow very fast. Do you feel optimistic or pessimistic about the cheetah's future?

'Cheating Extinction' in Botswana

The Cheetah – the fastest land animal in the world – can run at speeds of 110 kph. It's the fifth largest cat and one of the most beautiful. But the cheetah is in deadly danger. Its habitat is being destroyed as trees are cut down for wood, or mines are built to extract the region's minerals. Many animals are killed by hunters, and their skins are sold illegally around the world. Large numbers of cats are also shot every year by local farmers because they think that their animals are being attacked by the cheetah population. Thankfully, however, there are people fighting to save the cheetah and the rest of Africa's wildlife, such as Cheetah Conservation Botswana (CCB), an NGO operating in Botswana.

A key part of the CCB's work is to provide education about the cheetah for the local population. Several cheetahs have been rescued and are being looked after by the organisation. The public are then invited to see, touch and feed the animals to see what they are really like. The hope is that learning about cheetahs will stop local people being afraid of the animals. A second part of their work is scientific. Areas where the cheetahs live are carefully searched every day and the movements of the animals are entered into a database. Getting this scientific evidence is an important part of the NGO's work, alongside the usual charitable activities such as fundraising.

Nevertheless, the cheetah is in a race against time, and it is one that they are in danger of losing, despite their legendary speed. The population of cheetahs has fallen so much that there are only 10,000 left in the wild. It is now thought that they are in serious danger of extinction. Cheetahs only live for about eight years and usually have about four or five cubs every time the females give birth. But very few of these cubs become adults. Even in captivity, ⅓ of cubs die before they are one month old. This is very bad news for an animal that is quickly becoming yet another of the world's most endangered species.

50

Grammar

4 Look at the yellow verbs in the text. Complete the grammar rule. Then match the verbs to uses a–d.

> **The passive**
>
> **Form**
> verb _____ + _____ (e.g. *broken*, *grown*).
> use the preposition __ when you name the agent
>
> **Use**
> a to describe a common opinion, without saying exactly who believes it.
> b when it's obvious who did the action (e.g. some actions are only done by the police, doctors, the government.)
> c to describe a process.
> d to report news, to focus on the things affected.

5 Underline four more examples of the passive in the text.

AB p. 102 Ex. 4 ▶

> **Tip**
> The passive is also used in scientific writing to avoid using *I / we*.
> *The movements of the animals are entered into a database.*

6 Describe pictures A–D using the passive.

Guess what work the volunteers do with the cheetahs.

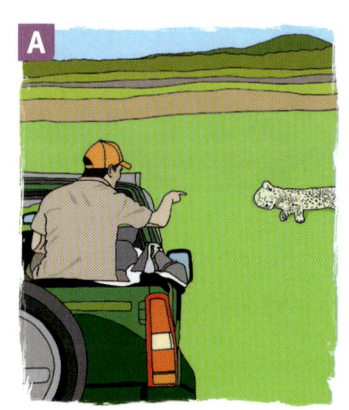

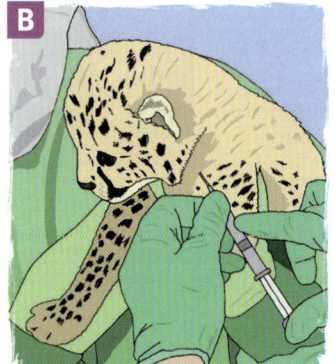

> *This cheetah's been injured. Maybe it's had an accident.*

Listening

7 🔊 4.12 Listen and match part 1 of an interview to the correct photo, A–C on p. 50. In pairs, what do remember about James' job and his family? Did he enjoy volunteering?

8 🔊 4.13 Guess if 1–7 are true (T) or false (F). Listen to part 2 to check.

1 James mostly taught teenagers. ___
2 Before arriving, James knew that the schools didn't have many resources. ___
3 There are many dangerous animals in Botswana. ___
4 He took the snake out of the classroom. ___
5 He really suffered from the weather. ___
6 He tries to get money for African schools. ___
7 He thinks Botswana has a very similar culture to the UK. ___

> **Remember?**
> *During* is a preposition. It's followed by a noun, not a subject + verb.
> *During his stay, he recorded his adventures in a blog.*
> *I didn't do anything during the holidays.*

Pronunciation

9 🔊 4.13 Look at the audioscript on p. 110. Is the pronunciation of the words in yellow the same (S) or different (D)? Listen to check.

Speaking

10 📄 In pairs, get a card from your teacher. Role-play the conversation.

Unit 4   51

4D Reality TV ruined my life!

Speaking

1 In threes, match four programme types to photos A–D. Have you ever been hooked on a TV show? Any you hate? Tell the class one interesting thing you learned about each other.

I never used to miss a single episode of The Sopranos.

a cartoon   a chat show   a documentary
a drama   the news   a reality show
a quiz show   a sitcom   a soap opera

Listening

2 **4.14** Listen to four people. In pairs, match each speaker to their favourite TV show from ex 1. What else did you understand about each one?

Heinz ☐   Natalie ☐   Bethany ☐   Alberto ☐

3 Listen again, then compare in pairs. How much more did you understand this time? Who was easiest/hardest to understand? Why?

Grammar

4 Complete what each person said. Check your answers in **4.14** on page 110. Notice the schwa /ə/.

1 If I hadn't been a *Simpsons* fan, I...
2 If I had been born in Australia, I...
3 If I'd applied for the show, I...
4 If I'd never watched *Mad Men*, I...

5 Read the grammar and complete the rule.

Mixed conditionals

Use the Second conditional for hypothetical situations, present and future.
If I were rich, I would travel round the world.

Use the Third conditional to hypothesise about the past.
If I hadn't gone to that party last year, I wouldn't have met my boyfriend.

We can also mix conditionals to hypothesise about the past and its effect on the present:
If the past had been different, life would be different today.

If + Past Perfect / Past Simple, *would* + *be* + past participle

AB p. 103 Ex. 2 ▶

6 Read about Caetano. Make five more mixed conditionals about him.

If Caetano had taken the role in the TV show, he'd be rich and famous today.

When he was 16, Caetano, who was tall and good-looking, was offered a role in a TV soap opera. He turned it down because he didn't like the character. But now the actor who did take the role is one of the biggest TV stars in Brazil. Caetano was never offered another role, and now he's 23 and works in a bank.

Tip

Many adjectives work in pairs: *nice and clean, tall and thin, cold and wet,* etc.
Make sure your room is clean and tidy.

Reading

7 In pairs, read the introduction to the interview. Cover the rest, and read it one question at a time. Guess Dean's answer before reading to check. How near were your guesses to his answers?

8 Look at the yellow words in the text. Can you express these idiomatic phrases?

> *I think this one means something like 'I left very quietly.'*

9 If Dean hadn't gone on *Big Brother*, how would his life be different now? Think about: his social life, music, home life and career.

> *If Dean hadn't gone on Big brother, his life would be very different today.*

How Big Brother ruined my life

What happens after Big Brother and contestants have to return home? Will their lives ever be 'normal' again? John Walsh asks Dean O'Loughlin from Big Brother 2

How did you feel in the days after leaving the 'Big Brother' house?
Because I came third, I sort of slipped away fairly unnoticed. That was good for me because the whole instant fame thing did my head in. The shock of it was quite intense. Being recognised everywhere you go, not being able to have a drink without being bothered and asked questions….

Everyone remembers you playing the guitar incessantly in the 'Big Brother' house. Did you get snapped up by a record company?
I didn't really think the TV show would launch my music career… but it surprised me to find it did the complete opposite. Suddenly I was seen as a bit of a joke, as a reality TV star trying to have a musical career. I mean, I've been in a band since I was 16, I had a deal with A&M records, we've had albums. I've been trying to have a musical career for 20 years! But Big Brother killed it stone dead.

You married your girlfriend Vanessa a few months after leaving the house. Did your relationship suffer because of 'Big Brother'?
It was a lot harder for her than it was for me… when we're out together, she still has to deal with it. People recognise me and suddenly I'm someone and she's less than no one, just this person on my arm. No one's talking to her. No one's shaking her hand. It really upsets the balance of your relationship, when you're no longer equal parts – in other people's eyes that is.

Did you make much money out of 'Big Brother'?
Not really. With the PAs [public appearances] and interviews, I probably made enough to afford to take a year off and not work – but the difficult thing was to think what do I do then? You can't go back to a normal job… because, unless you're driving around in a limousine or appearing on TV, you're seen as a failure.

Have you any advice for people auditioning for Big Brother 5?
Yes. It's really simple. Just don't.

Speaking

10 Ten contestants on a reality TV show spend ten weeks on a desert island. Each is allowed to take one personal object with them. However, after five weeks, not everybody is happy with their object. In groups, imagine what they're saying about the objects below. Try to use second, third and mixed conditionals.

Essential phrases
If I'd known…
If I'd thought about it a bit more carefully…
If I'd been a bit cleverer…
Why on earth did…
If you'd asked me…
If I were you…

4E My avatar and me

Speaking

1 **4.15** In groups, compare your top three ways of using the Internet. Go to Word Bank 19, p. 74.

> **A:** *I guess mine would be chatting, finding and checking information and downloading music and films – legally of course!*

Reading

2 Do you know anything about Second Life? Skim the text to check. What else did you learn? Imagine two advantages and two disadvantages of learning English in SL.

> Maynard Farrell owns and manages a language school in São Paolo, Brazil. They hold English classes on Sunday evenings in Second Life, where people learn from home. **Second Life** (SL) is a virtual world, created by Linden Lab. In SL, users create an *avatar*, which is their representation in the world. Some avatars look like their human creators, while others look like animals or fictional characters. In a SL class, avatars can speak to and interact directly with other students through a microphone and see a virtual whiteboard on a screen. They take part in a lesson as if they are on TV, except that they are one of the characters!

3 Maynard was asked these questions. Can you guess his answers?

1 How is a 'virtual' lesson better or worse than a lesson in 'the real world'?
2 What kind of avatars do you have in the class?
3 Do people usually look like their avatars?
4 Since the success of the film, are more people interested in avatars?
5 What do users see on the screen during an online lesson?
6 Are people more willing to communicate in a virtual learning environment?

4 Read and complete the interview with five of the questions from ex 3.

5 Cover the text. In pairs remember all you can from the interview.

My Second Life

A REEC online interview/podcast with Maynard Farrell of UP Language Consultants, Brazil

A _____

They see the teacher, the other students, the resources we use to present and practice the language topic of the day, things like PowerPoint slides, texts, pictures and any other props that the teacher feels may be useful.

B _____

On one hand it's **easier** than going to a normal school in real life, because you don't even have to leave your sitting room; you just fly or teleport to class. On the other hand, it's **harder** for students because they also have to learn how to control their avatars before they can begin learning English. That's **the most difficult** thing. **It's much simpler** to just walk into a classroom, sit down and open your book than it is to learn how to manipulate an avatar. It took me about 3 months to really learn properly.

C _____

It seems that people take on a kind of role when they become a resident in SL. This usually makes them **more interactive and communicative**, unafraid to take risks or guess the meaning of utterances or words. However, you never know "who" is really behind the Avatar! You know it's a person, but it may not be the person you think it is. For example, we could not give a student a test using SL. How would we know who is truly operating the avatar and answering the questions?

D _____

Well, I have already given classes to a Hungarian Snow dog. The **stangest** avatar was definitely an android from some weird planet. But from an SL point of view, teaching a dog or an android is **as easy as** teaching a human being.

E _____

Usually people create a 'second' life, not a 'first' life. Their second life would be a kind of alter ego so to speak. Something they are "not" in real life perhaps. I have 2 avatars, one looks like me, is a man and is called Maynard Ninetails, the other is a beautiful woman called Klockgin Kowalski who looks like a Hollywood actress. Some people's avatars are surprisingly lifelike and the resemblances to the real people are incredibly similar.

6 Look at the **yellow** words in the text. What are the rules for making 1) comparatives, 2) superlatives? Which structure means two things are equal?

Listening

7 (4.16) Listen to four Second Lifers describing their avatar for a survey. Match each speaker (1–4) to their avatar (A–D).

1 ☐ 2 ☐ 3 ☐ 4 ☐

8 Match the phrases to the speakers 1–4. Listen again to check. Who was the easiest / hardest to understand? Who's most similar to you?

a Most of my friends have avatars that are *just* as ridiculous as this! ☐
b Using the virtual world isn't *quite* as easy as I'd expected ☐
c He's *slightly* more handsome than I am. ☐
d It's *far* more exciting than real life. ☐

Grammar

9 Complete gaps 1–4 with yellow words from ex 8.

Making comparisons	
1 Use these words with the comparative	**Meaning**
This computer is *much* / ¹_____ quicker than the old one.	A lot
The morning flight is *a bit* / ²_____ more expensive than the evening one.	A little
2 Use these words with *as ... as*	
My old teacher was *nowhere near* / *not nearly* as good as my new one.	Not at all
The four star hotel is ³_____ as good as the three star one.	Exactly
The new exam isn't ⁴_____ as difficult as the old one.	Almost

AB p. 104 Ex. 5 ▶

10 Play AVATAR. Get a card from your teacher.

Speaking

11 In pairs, design and quickly sketch an avatar for your teacher to use in an online SL English lesson. Swap sketches with another pair. Compare the avatar with your teacher. Are they similar? Vote and decide the class favourite.

4F The Internet generation

Speaking

1 In groups, compare childhood today and 40 years ago (before TV and computers). Do you all agree?

1. What kind of games did children use to play?
2. How similar is that to the way kids spend their free time today?
3. Was it better to be a child in the past or a child today?

My parents say they used to play outside a lot more than me.

Listening

2 🔊 4.17 Do you think children today are more resourceful because of the Internet and computers? Go to Word Bank 5, p. 67.

Possibly, but they certainly don't write or read in the same way.

3 🔊 4.18 Serena Hoppe is researching teenagers' use of technology. Do you think these sentences will be true or false? Listen to Part 1 of the interview and check.

1. Serena worries about her children's computer use.
2. She thinks childhood was better in the past.
3. She thinks computers are as bad as TV.
4. She thinks it's OK for boys to play violent computer games.

4 🔊 4.19 Before listening to the rest of the interview, guess how these sentences end. Listen and check.

1. Children are very resourceful at _____.
2. Like most teenagers, he spends most of his time _____.
3. Some people say modern children cannot communicate because _____.
4. I think teenagers today are better _____.
5. We mustn't be snobbish about online _____.
6. There is false information in _____.

Reading

5 In fives, each student find two mistakes in the essay:
- **A** with articles.
- **B** with tenses.
- **C** with punctuation.
- **D** with word order.
- **E** with prepositions.

Think back to your happiest childhood memory. Was it playing in the beach or exploring the countryside with your friends? Perhaps it was a party or playing in the park football. One thing I am sure of is that it wasn't playing a computer game.

Of course, this is partly due to parents concerns about their children. The increased number of methods of communication have given us more news than ever. As a result, many parents hear so many terrible stories that they keep their kids indoors. They don't let them play outside with the freedom that children enjoyed on the past.

Look at social networking sites. Although the average teenager might have hundreds of online 'friends', how many real friends do they have. People they actually spend time with? Very few. This is all the fault of technology. Online contacts have become a substitute for real friendship.

Don't get me wrong. We all know computers have made people's lives easier in many ways. For instance, its now simple to find travel information or book a holiday online. That's quite difficult in the past. However, we do need to consider how has technology affected modern life for the worse.

To sum up, computers have made people more nervous, more stressful and less sociable than they were years ago. After we are accepting this fact, we can start taking action to reduce the negative effects of the computers on our lives, and those of our children.

Remember?
how to use apostrophes?
My brother's car is a Fiat.
My brothers' friends are great fun!

Grammar

6 Match rules 1 to 3 to the yellow examples in the text.

Linking phrases

1 An adverb

actually anyway apparently certainly
curiously hopefully however ideally
ironically thankfully

connects two independent sentences, or introduces a change of direction:
However, we need to consider …

2 A conjunction

although before this/that even though
now that once rather than

begins a clause which is dependent on the information that follows:
Even though I like computers, my parents don't want me to buy one

3 A phrase

all in all as a result of… for example To sum up

introduces a conclusion, or exemplifies what has previously been said.
To sum up…

7 Now replace each of the yellow highlighted words in the essay in ex. 5 with words from the box, without changing anything else in the sentence.

> for example   nevertheless   even though
> because of   consequently   all in all

AB p. 105 Ex. 1 ▶

Speaking

8 Read paragraph 1 of this 'For and Against' essay. Then, work in two groups. Group A, write paragraph 2 (For). Group B, write paragraph 3 (Against).

Technology has destroyed childhood

Children today know more about computers and technology than any previous generation. Where their parents were excited by a digital watch or an arcade game like PacMan, kids today have hundreds of different gadgets to play with. They use technology all the time, and this has affected the way they do their schoolwork, how they spend their free time, and most of all, what they do with their friends.

9 Swap paragraphs with another pair. Correct each other's work using the different rules in ex 6.

10 Write a conclusion to your essay.

Unit 4   57

4 Revision

4A 1 Read the survey and add two questions you'd like to ask the class. Then mingle and answer, asking follow-up questions too.

Find someone who...	Name
1 has been to three countries in one day.	_____
2 ate out last week.	_____
3 has their own website.	_____
4 has been studying / working hard this week.	_____
5 has met a famous person.	_____
6 has not learnt to drive.	_____
7 had a crazy hairstyle when they were younger.	_____
8 has an unusual hobby.	_____
9 has brought at least 2 gadgets to class today.	_____
10 is going to upload something this week.	_____
11 has seen an endangered species in the wild.	_____
12 has appeared on TV.	_____
13 _____	_____
14 _____	_____

2 In pairs, imagine you're at a music festival. You've just been to different stages and seen your favourite bands. **A** you were disappointed. **B** you loved your gig. Role-play your conversation. Include the topics in the box. Try to use all the useful phrases.

> musicians   clothes   lighting
> set list   atmosphere   encore

> Wow!   Really?   You know what I mean.
> Uh-huh.   No way!   Cool.

Song: *Boulevard of Broken Dreams* by Green Day

To find the words, google *lyric* + the song title.

To find the video, google *video* + the song title and singer.

Make sure you use only legal websites.

4B 3 4.20 Listen to four dialogues and circle a or b.
1 The woman didn't enjoy the party because
   a she didn't know anybody there.
   b there were only a few people there.
2 The man complains about his phone because
   a it has a large number of complicated functions.
   b the design is too modern and trendy.
3 The problem with the biscuits is that they
   a are too sweet.
   b contain too much salt.
4 Ricky
   a is going out with a girl he met online.
   b isn't going out with anyone at the moment.

4 Listen again and complete the sentences.
1 We were in this huge club with _____.
2 Give it to me. I know _____.
3 Yeah, they're ready! Do you _____?
4 Give it a little time and _____.

5 Look at 4.20 on p. 110. Find four words that have been changed from US to UK English.

4C 6 In pairs, look at the photos for 30 seconds. Then close your books and compare the two volunteers. Which job would you prefer to do?

7 Role-play a conversation for both photos: **A** you're the volunteer in the first picture. **B** you're the volunteer in the second picture.

8 Do ex 3 in Word Bank 18 on p. 74.

9 In threes, play WHAT'S HAPPENED? Get a card from your teacher.

4D 10 In pairs, read the sentence and complete the mixed conditional.

1 'We were late getting to the airport and they've bumped us off our flight!
   If we'd arrived a bit earlier, we'd be sitting on the plane by now!

2 'I've eaten eight courses and I don't feel well at all now. If _____.'

3 'I met Ximena when I was in Colombia and now we're engaged! If _____.'

4 'I broke my leg in a skiing accident and I have to stay in hospital for three weeks! If _____.'

5 'I saw the job in the newspaper last week, and now I have an interview! If _____.'

6 'We're at the hotel but there are no vacancies, so we can't stay here. If _____.'

11 In pairs, role-play the conversations. **A** is the person speaking in 1, 3 and 5. **B** is the person speaking in 2, 4 and 6. How long can you keep the conversation going?

4E 12 In pairs, compare some websites that you know until you can agree and complete 1–5. Swap partners and compare ideas. Any disagreements?

1 This _____ is much worse than _____

2 I use _____ just as often as _____

3 I don't use _____ nearly as much as _____

4 _____ isn't quite as popular as _____

5 I think _____ is slightly better than _____

4F 13 In pairs, look at the text and find 2

1 punctuation errors
2 spelling errors
3 errors with articles
4 errors with word order
5 preposition errors

> ### Electronic books start to kindle enthusiasm
>
> In 2007, online e-tailer Amazon launched Kindle, the companys own electronic reader for books. It's as thin as a magazine and you can save almost 1,500 books on it. Battery is good too and can last as long as 7 days, so you don't need to worry that the power might disappear just as you get to the exiting bit.
>
> This is all part of a huge movement to abandon old-fashioned paper books. Allready in California, Governor Arnold Schwarzenegger is replacing some course books from downloads. Its only a question of time before other school systems start to follow his example.
>
> However, there are disadvantages at losing the traditional book. You cannot write down in an e-book answers, even if you can write comments. Also, many people prefer reading on paper to looking at a screen. And of course, the books are more than just text on paper. For instance, if you give a book as a gift, you give a physical object that someone can keep forever. I can't imagine how would a child feel if you gave them a download as a present instead.

14 What do you feel about the debate in ex 13?

15 In fours, look back at one unit each to see what you can remember. Choose:

1 a text you enjoyed
2 a word or phrase that you don't have in your language
3 a picture that makes you laugh
4 some grammar you now feel more confident with.

16 (4.21) Go to Word Bank 20 p. 75. Listen and chant the 15 voiced consonants.

Go to **Writing 4** p. 63 ▶

UNIT 4   59

Writing 1 — A formal email

1 Read the email and complete the summary.

> Mi-Sun wants to study ¹ _____. She asks for more information about the ² _____ _____, about opportunities to get ³ _____ _____ and a place to live.

Email:

ᵃDear Ms Jenkins

I am writing to you to ᵇrequest some information ᶜregarding the International Catering Course at Greenbrook College. I saw your college advertised in *International News Magazine*. ᵈI wonder if you would be able to answer a few questions for me?

I am ᵉcurrently in my last year at High School here in Seoul and I should receive my Korean High School Diploma at the end of this year. I saw on your website that, ᶠin addition to this, I would need to pass the IELTS exam. Could you send me some details about this? What mark would I need to ᵍobtain? Do you know whether and where the exam can be taken in Korea?

I also saw on your website that there is a ʰlarge number of restaurants and hotels whose managers and chefs have studied at your college. Do you arrange work experience for your students as part of the course? That would be very interesting for me in the future.

Finally, the website also mentioned that there is accommodation available for international students, but I was unable to ⁱaccess any of this online. Could you send me some ʲfurther information about this too, please?

Thank you very much for your time.

ᵏBest regards
Mi-sun Lee

2 True or false? Re-read the email to check.

Rules
In formal emails and letters:
1 sentences are often longer than in informal texts. T/F
2 don't use contractions. T/F
3 use short forms, like *thanks* or *ad*. T/F
4 writers tend to avoid phrasal verbs. T/F
5 never use direct questions. T/F
6 use lots of modals verbs like *would* and *could*. T/F

Writing tip
Avoid spoken language forms in formal writing.

3 Match yellow words, a-k, to these informal equivalents.

about	c	all the best		as well as		ask for		at the moment	
could you		get		get to		hi		lot		more	

4 Circle the more formal options.
1 I would like to *find out* / *(learn more)* about…
2 I hope you will be able to *accept* / *say* 'yes' to me on your course.
3 I am *unable to* / *can't* attend on…
4 I have *loads of* / *substantial* experience…
5 I would be *delighted* / *happy* to attend an interview.
6 I *believe* / *think* I am ideally qualified for…
7 I *can't wait for* / *look forward to* your reply.
8 I really enjoy sports *like* / *such as* swimming…

5 Write a formal email in reply to this ad from *Escape* magazine.
- Write four paragraphs:
  1st: Why are you writing?
  2nd: Why are you are interested in the course?
  3rd: Ask for more information (class size? hours per day? own camera? etc.)
  4th: Ask about prices and accommodation in Vancouver.
- Check you
  – follow the rules in ex 2
  – use appropriate phrases from exs 3 and 4
  – begin and end formally.
- Swap emails with a partner to check. Underline anything you think might be wrong, then give it back.
- Give your final version to your teacher.

> **Apply for our Travel photography course!**
>
> Learn how to take great pictures – in just four weeks! Courses start in Vancouver on the 1st Monday of every month.
>
> For more information, email Lisa Patel at
> lpatel@travelphotographycourse.co.uk

An anecdote — Writing 2

1 Read the story and order the pictures 1st to 6th. What would you have said and done next?

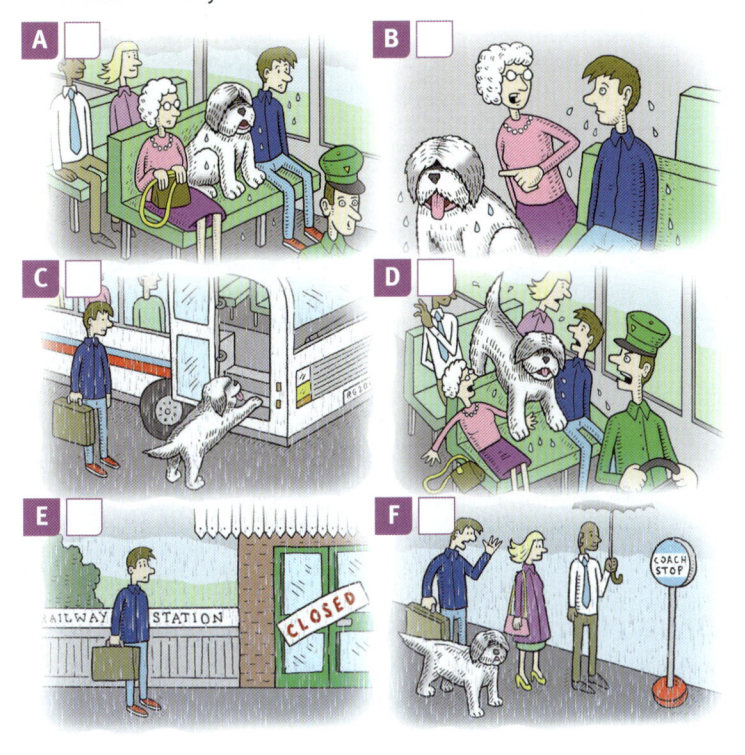

A B C D E F

Writing tip

1 'Set the scene' with the past continuous. Begin with phrases like '(*Once/A few years ago*), *when I was* (*living in / going to*) …'. Use the past perfect to say what had happened before and the past simple to list events, one by one.

2 Keep a record of useful new story-telling phrases and swap lists with other students. Always check each other's work too <u>before and after</u> the teacher corrects it to learn as much as possible from each other.

An unusual journey

Once I was travelling home to see my parents and I had to get the train at a remote railway station. When I got there, it was raining really hard and the station was closed. *Apparently*, it had been raining for days and several rivers had flooded! So, I decided to get the coach *instead*. When I got to the bus station, there was just me, four other people and this dog. Everyone was just standing around, waiting, and complaining about the weather.

When the coach arrived, it was really crowded, but I managed to get on, just after the dog. The dog was really big, very hairy, and incredibly wet. *As soon as* it got on the train, it *suddenly* went crazy. It was jumping on people, and making a terrible noise. I looked around but nobody said anything, so *in the end*, the driver shouted at it. *At that point*, it went quiet and fell asleep on the next seat, between me and this elderly lady. It was horrible, sitting next to this huge wet dog for the whole journey. It kept waking up and looking at me!

Eventually, after four hours on the coach, we got to my stop. *Just as* I was getting out of my seat and leaving, I heard the lady say, in a very angry voice, "Excuse me, aren't you going to take your dog with you?" And it was true: I was the only person left on the coach from my stop!

---

2 Read Writing tip 1. Underline the five actions 'in progress' in paragraph 1 of the story.

3 Read tip 2. Complete the sentences with two of the phrases in brackets. Then check your answers with the yellow words.

1 _____ I got to the main entrance, I saw lots of reporters outside, so I went round to the back door _____. (as soon as, astonishingly, instead)

2 We had been waiting to see the stars for hours, so _____ we decided to leave, but _____ we were going, Tom Cruise walked out of the door! (as long as, eventually, just as)

3 They had hoped to climb four mountains in the range but _____ they only managed to climb one of them. _____ the weather was just too dangerous to try any of the others. (apparently, fortunately, in the end)

4 I was in the living room when _____ all the lights went out. I went round the house checking the electricity but nothing was working. _____ I realised that something bad was going on. (at that point, occasionally, suddenly)

4 Write an 'Unusual journey' anecdote, preferably one that's true.

1 Quickly draft your whole story in note form. Have a break, then:
- Divide your ideas into four 'paragraphs'.
- Write paragraph 1 in full. Set the scene, following tip 1.
- Complete the other three paragraphs.
- Check you have included at least five story telling phrases and underline them.

2 Swap texts with a partner to read through and check. Write a positive comment too, eg *Amazing – did this really happen? / Very funny. I had a similar experience myself.* Then give / send it to your teacher with the comment still on it.

Writing 3 — A biography

As good as art gets?

Diego Rivera (1886–1959) is one of Latin America's most famous artists. He painted wonderful portraits and giant historical murals. Some are so big that they cover entire walls!

Rivera and his twin brother Jose Carlos were born in Guanajuato, Mexico. Tragically, Jose died before their second birthday. The family then moved to Mexico City, where young Diego started to draw and paint. Later he went on to study art in Paris and Madrid.

Rivera's paintings show people and animals in simple scenes. However, these images are often complex and political. Rivera was a communist throughout his life and his pictures tell stories about colonialism, society and the poor.

He is also famous for having relationships with many beautiful women, especially the great artist Frida Kahlo. She was 22 years younger than him. Over thirty years, they were married, divorced and then remarried.

Today, we should remember him for his great works of art. Most photos don't show how large the images really are, or the amazing colours that he used. He is, without doubt, one of the great modern masters.

---

1 Read tip 1. Quickly read and match the yellow 'topic' sentences in the biography to paragraph contents a–e. Then read the whole text to check.

  a early life
  b personal life
  c why he's still important
  d type of art
  e who he is

2 How many times does the writer use *I, me, my,* or *In my opinion?* Why? Read tip 2 to check.

3 Read tip 3. Cut 20 more unnecessary words from this paragraph.

Writing tip

1 In a report or wiki, begin each paragraph with a 'topic sentence' to tell your reader what it will contain.
2 Don't use the first person when you are writing factual information.
3 Keep sentences short. Don't repeat subjects, verbs or prepositional phrases.
4 Don't just translate from your language. Try to 'Think In English' and Keep Ideas Simple (TIE and KIS!) Remember mistakes you've made before. Re-read each paragraph aloud without translating. Does it sound like clear, simple English?

During his career, Rivera worked in Mexico and ~~he worked in~~ the USA. He painted some murals in San Francisco and he painted others in Detroit too. However, his most famous mural in the USA is a mural that no longer exists. In 1933, he created 'Man at the Crossroads' for the Rockefeller Center in New York City. When it was completed, the newspapers were furious because Rivera had included a picture of the communist leader Lenin in the mural. At that time, the USA was very anti-communist, so people in America were shocked and they were angry that he had included this image of Lenin in the work. In the end, the mural was removed and it was replaced.

---

4 <u>In your language</u>, quickly research someone famous on the net. Make notes for a short biography in 5 paragraphs, in the same order as ex 1. Think of a topic sentence for each paragraph.

5 In English, turn your notes into a clear, simple biography of about 180 words:

- Follow tips 2 to 4.
- Swap drafts with another student to check then give it to your teacher.

A review — Writing 4

The Winter Queen by Boris Akunin

The Winter Queen is a historical whodunit set in 19th century Moscow. It was a huge hit in Russia and it's soon going to be made into a movie.

The Winter Queen is the story of Erast Fandorin, a young detective who is investigating a mysterious death. It follows his adventures as a murder leads him to a mysterious organisation known as Azazel (the original Russian name of the novel).

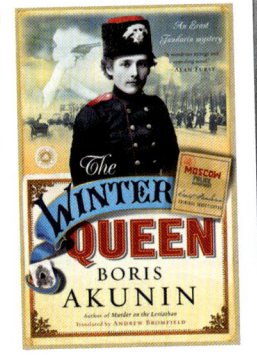

What's very original is that the main character is not a genius like Sherlock Holmes. He makes mistakes and he gets into trouble. What's also surprising is that the book is often really funny, unlike a lot of detective fiction!

I started reading the book yesterday morning and I couldn't put it down. It's terrific, funny and full of great dialogue! If you like mystery, action, and adventure in the spirit of Arthur Conan Doyle and Jules Verne, this is the book for you.

Rasheda

Star Trek

Star Trek was one of the biggest movies of 2009, based on the famous 60s Sci-Fi show. It is the latest adventure for the crew of the Starship Enterprise as they explore amazing alien planets in the far future.

It's the story of an alien, Nero, who can destroy whole planets. The young crew of the Enterprise have to do everything they can to stop him, even though they have only just finished their training!

What was really interesting in the film was the relationship between the young Spock (Zachary Pinto) and Kirk (Chris Pine). In the TV series they were friends, but in the new film they don't like each other. That was great because you couldn't predict what was going to happen next!

I went to see the film with my boyfriend and he absolutely loved it, but I can't say I really enjoyed it. The best thing about it were the special effects, and if you like science fiction, you'll love this! But I'm more into rom-coms myself!

Cintia

---

1 Read the reviews. Answer the questions in Writing tip 1.

Writing tip 1

Answer these questions when you write a review. Copy the order:

1. What kind of book / film is it?
2. Where's it set?
3. What's the plot? Just say (but don't give away the ending).
4. Who are the main characters?
5. Did the reviewer like it? Why (not)?

2 True or false? Re-read the reviews to check.

Writing tip 2

A review is a semi-formal piece of writing. In semi-formal writing:

1. don't use contractions. T/F
2. you can use exclamation marks (!). T/F
3. don't use personal language like *I*, *me*, *In my opinion*. T/F
4. use spoken English phrases like *full of* or *be into*. T/F
5. talk to the reader directly as 'you'. T/F
6. try to avoid phrasal verbs. T/F

3 Read tip 3. Underline 2 cleft sentences in each review. Does your language have cleft sentences?

Writing tip 3

For emphasis, start sentences with key phrases + *is / was*. These are 'cleft sentences'.

The best thing about the book was the ending.

What I liked was the descriptions of everyday life.

What surprised me was the number of characters.

The person who recommended it to me is a big fan of the author.

4 Order the green words to make cleft sentences.

1. what enjoyed really I was the start of the film.
2. for bit best the me was when the main character meets the villain in a deserted harbour.
3. like Harry who Potter people are going to love this movie.
4. wanted what I was to learn more about nineteenth-century Moscow.
5. about film best the thing the was the special effects.

5 Write a review of a book or film you know (about 160 words). Encourage (or discourage) your reader to read / see it.

- Use the model in tip 1 above.
- Write the review. Include at least two cleft sentences. Avoid repeating any adjectives.
- Swap drafts with another student. Check it for errors. Does it tell you enough to persuade you?
- Give it to your teacher.

Word Bank 1   Collocations

1 🔊 **1.1** Listen to the story. Then match the collocations with pictures 1–9. Listen again to check.

- apply for jobs ☐
- be heavily in debt ☐
- be sick to death of sth ☐
- be under a lot of stress ☐
- course be over ☑
- do work experience ☐
- send out CVs ☐
- walk into ☐
- a well-paid job ☐

2 Which type of word is used in each collocation? Which four are phrasal verbs?

Well-paid is an adjective, job is a noun…

3 In pairs, re-tell Deng's story.

▶ 1A p.4

Picture captions:
1. At last… The good news…
2. The bad news?…
3. So…
4. and…
5. sure…
6. … at a big company
7. But…
8. So in the end…
9. still, three months later And…

Tip

It's vital to remember words together, not alone. *Collocations* are two or more words that always combine together, e.g. verb + noun (**do the shopping**), verb + preposition (**mad about**), noun + preposition (**boss of a company**), adjective + noun (**a tall man**), etc.

Good dictionaries give multiple examples, or you can google to find more. Learning collocations definitely leads to greater fluency!

4 🔊 **1.12** Match the *get* collocations to pictures 10–17. Listen and check.

- ☐ get + object + -ing = start
  get me thinking
- ☐ get + infinitive = manage / have an opportunity
  get to stay in
- ☐ get + direct object = obtain
  get a drink
- ☐ get + adverb / preposition = movement
  get away
- ☐ get + comparative = become
  get older
- ☐ get + noun = catch (a disease)
  get malaria
- ☐ get + direct object = receive
  get a text
- ☐ get + location / + preposition + noun = arrive
  get to the port

5 What other meanings of *get* do you know? Which grammatical pattern from ex 4 do they follow?

It can mean 'understand' as in 'I don't get it'.

▶ 1E p.12

64

Phrasal verbs — Word Bank 2

1 🔊 1.3 Listen and match the phrasal verbs with pictures 1–10. Listen again to check.

- break up ☐
- bring up ☐
- fall out ☐
- get on with ☐
- go out with ☐
- grow up ☐
- live up to ☐
- move out ☐
- take after 2
- tell off ☐

1B p.6

2 🔊 1.15 Listen and match the phrasal verbs with pictures 11–19. Listen again to check.

- ☐ eat out
- ☐ call up
- ☐ figure out
- ☐ find out
- ☐ fit in
- ☐ get by
- ☐ hang around
- ☐ run out of
- ☐ turn up

1F p.14

3 Match these more formal words with their phrasal verb equivalent from 1 and 2.

arrive   contact   discover   resemble   separate   survive   understand

1R p.16

65

Word Bank 3 — Words for feelings

1 🔊 1.6 Match the adjectives with pictures 1–12. Listen and check.

- [ ] appalling
- [ ] astonished
- [ ] confused
- [ ] delighted
- [ ] down
- [ ] excited
- [ ] exhausted
- [ ] go red
- [ ] go white
- [ ] nervous
- [ ] shocked
- [ ] stressed out

2 In pairs, remember a time when you felt each of these emotions.

I've never been down for long as I'm very positive, but I was a bit depressed when my grandma died.

1C p.8

Tip

interesting or *interested*?

-ing adjectives describe *what* or *who* causes an emotion. *This exercise is really confusing.*

-ed adjectives describe the experience of this emotion. *I'm so confused.*

All the *-ed* adjectives on this page have *-ing* forms except *stressed* (*stressful*) and *delighted* (*delightful*).

Word Bank 4 — Intensifiers

Tip

Use adverbs like *extremely, incredibly, ridiculously* and *unbelievably* to intensify most adjectives except those which mean *completely* or *100%*, like *perfect* or *impossible*. With these 'extreme' adjectives use *absolutely, completely* or *totally*.

My tiny new laptop is absolutely ideal for travelling.

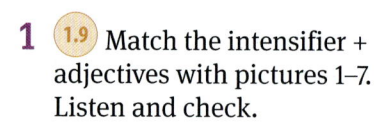

1 🔊 1.9 Match the intensifier + adjectives with pictures 1–7. Listen and check.

- [ ] absolutely astonished
- [ ] completely crazy
- [ ] extremely embarrassing
- [ ] incredibly intelligent
- [ ] ridiculously rich
- [ ] totally terrified
- [ ] unbelievably uncomfortable

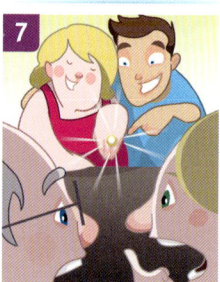

2 In pairs, share your own experiences of the adjectives on this page. Use an intensifier with each adjective.

We had an incredibly boring Maths teacher at secondary school. He was unbelievably dull.

1D p.10

66

Adjective suffixes — Word Bank 5

1 🔊 2.1 Circle the adjectives in pictures 1–9. Listen and check.

1 ad**dic**tive, i**mag**inative, re**pe**titive
2 **end**less, **help**less, **use**less
3 **change**able, com**for**table, unfor**get**table
4 be... **care**ful, **pain**ful, **use**ful
5 not... **news**worthy, **note**worthy, **trust**worthy
6 **green**ish, **hell**ish, **self**ish
7 (not) en**vi**ronmental, **op**tional, pro**fes**sional
8 ad**ven**turous, **dan**gerous, **fu**rious
9 **ed**ible, **flex**ible, in**vis**ible

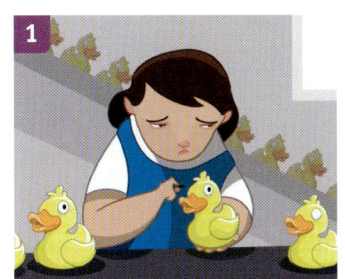

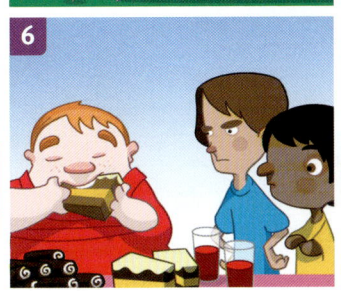

2 Can you identify the root of each word? Is the root a verb or a noun?

A: *The root of addictive is addict. It's a noun.*

▶ 2A p.18

3 🔊 4.17 Match the adjectives with pictures 10–17. Listen and check.

- ☐ (not) a**dap**table
- ☐ ef**fec**tive
- ☐ incompre**hen**sible
- ☐ re**source**ful
- ☐ **chat**ty
- ☐ **gen**erous
- ☐ i**ni**tial
- ☐ **snob**bish

4 Can you identify the root of each word? Is the root a verb or a noun?

▶ 4F p.56

Word Bank 6 — Negative prefixes

Tip

The most common way to make an adjective negative is by adding *un*: e.g. *untidy*, *unkind*.

You can also use
- dis → disappointed
- in → incorrect.

And for some adjectives beginning with *p, l, m* or *r*, use
- il + l → illogical
- im + p → improbable; im + m → immature
- ir + r → irrational

1 (2.3) Match the adjectives with pictures 1–9. Listen, check and repeat.

- illegal
- illegible
- impatient
- indirect
- irrelevant
- incomplete
- inedible
- disabled
- uninteresting

2 (2.4) Make the adjectives negative. Then listen and check. Does the negative prefix change the word stress?

__accurate   __honest   __moral   __regular   __satisfied
__adventurous   __literate   __polite   __responsible

2B p.20

Word Bank 7 — Reporting verbs

1 (2.10) Listen and match a–h to pictures 1–8.

	Less formal	More formal
a	ask	enquire
b	ask for	request
c	mention	raise
d	moan	complain
e	point out	highlight
f	reply	respond
g	say	state
h	tell	inform

2 In pairs, report the conversation, A as the man, B as the boss.

2C p.22

Tip

inform & *tell* have an indirect object:
He **informed us** of / **told us** the answer.
ask can be followed by an indirect object or not:
He **asked (me)** if I was going home.
The **other reporting verbs above** do not have an indirect object.

68

Money — Word Bank 8

1 🔊 2.12 Listen and read idioms 1–6. In pairs, express what they mean. Does your language have equivalent expressions?

1. **I'm broke**. I don't have a cent on me. 
2. In this job, you usually get paid **cash in hand**. 
3. I can't work full-time because of the children, but I do earn a bit of **money on the side**. 
4. Ever since the robots became really popular, we've been **making serious money**. 
5. I've lost my job and so we'll all have **to tighten our belts**. 
6. They were all involved in the robbery and everyone is going **to take a cut**.

2 🔊 2.13 Circle the word or phrase that matches each picture.

7. a grant / a loan / wages
8. hard up / starving / wealthy
9. a pension / sickness benefit / unemployment benefit
10. be overcharged / overdrawn / overpaid

➤ 2D p.24

3 Which one in each group do you associate with most?

A: *Wages. I've never had a salary or a grant. I've only ever worked at weekends.*

➤ 2R p.30

Noun forms — Word Bank 9

1 🔊 2.15 Match words 1–15 to pictures a–o. Listen, check and repeat.

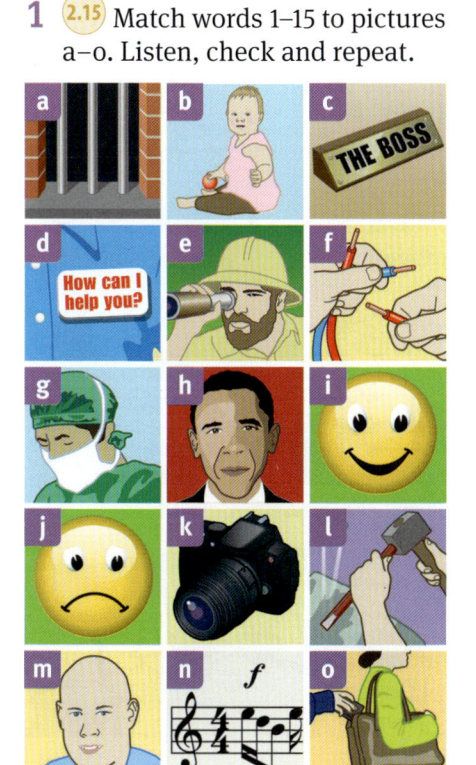

Adjective	Noun	Person
bald/balding	baldness	[1] a bald man
childish	childhood	[2] a child
criminal	crime	[3] a criminal
electric / electrical	electricity	[4] an electrician
(un)employed	(un)employment	[5] an employer / [6] employee
(un)explored	exploration	[7] an explorer
music / musical	music	[8] a musician
imprisoned	prison	[9] a prisoner
optimistic	optimism	[10] an optimist
pessimistic	pessimism	[11] a pessimist
photographic	photography / Photograph	[12] a photographer
presidential	presidency	[13] a president
sculpture	sculpture	[14] a sculptor
surgical	surgery	[15] a surgeon

2 Underline the words where the stress moves from the root. What are the pronunciation rules for suffixes *-ic* and *-tial*?

➤ 2E p.26

69

Word Bank 10 — Cars and driving

1 (2.20) Match the words to numbers 1–14. Listen and check.

accelerator   boot (US: *trunk*)   brake   clutch   disabled parking space   engine   gears / gearstick (US: *gear shift*)   handbrake   indicator   one-way street   pavement   sat-nav   steering wheel   tyres (US: *tires*)

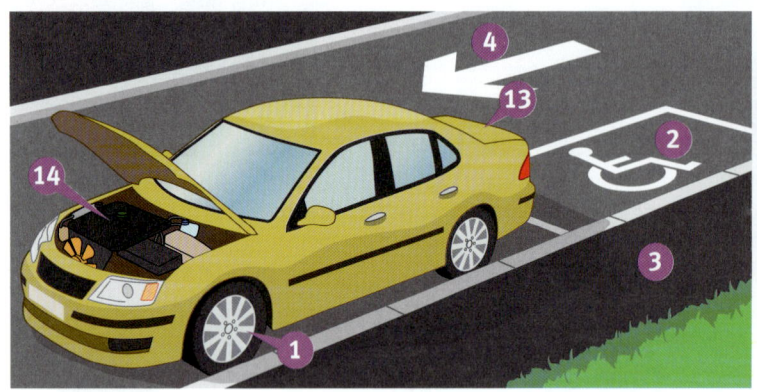

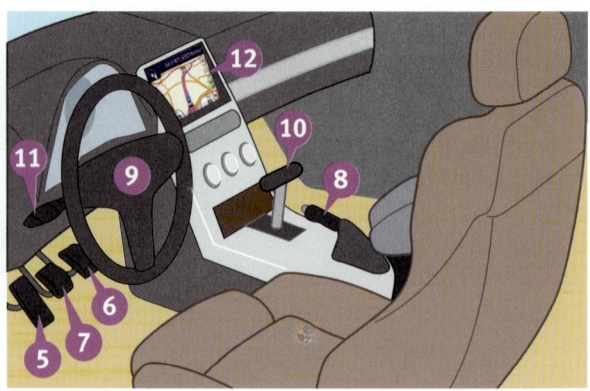

2 In pairs, A mime a word. B, say what your partner's doing.

  B: *You're starting the engine. Now you're taking off the handbrake.*

2F p.28

Word Bank 11 — Illnesses

1 (3.3) Listen and number the verbs 1–3.   cough   sneeze   sniff

2 (3.4) Listen to the story. Then match the words to pictures 1–11.

- check someone in (to hospital)
- a cold
- feel stiff
- a fever
- flu
- a headache
- a high temperature
- a hypochondriac
- a nurse
- a patient
- sore throat

Picture captions:
1 Keith's…always
2 One day…
3 also…
4 At first…
5 so…as usual…
6 terrible… and a…39°
7 Next morning…
8 sure…
9 So… At first/pretending
10 But… doctor… immediately
11 Now / real / happiest

3 In pairs, A explain the use of one item, 1–14. B, guess which one it is.

  A: *You use it to power the car.*

3 In pairs, tell the story, A as the narrator, then B as Keith.

3B p.34

Word + preposition — Word Bank 12

Tip
Be careful with these verbs:
I'm looking forward **to seeing** you tomorrow.
I can't get used **to living** without you.

1 (3.9) Listen and circle the adjective in pictures 1–6.

1	complain	special	worried	about
2	grateful	ready	responsible	for
3	allergic	desperate	married	to
4	based	hooked	keen	on
5	available	interested	involved	in
6	full	jealous	terrified	of

Test a partner on the prepositions.

A: *Based?*   **B:** *On. Jealous?*

2 (3.10) Match pictures 7–11 to a collocation. Listen and check.

verb + preposition	noun + preposition
bother about	advice for
dream of / about	effect on
invite to	expert in
specialise in	list of
suffer from	member of

3C p.36   3R p.44

The face and appearance — Word Bank 13

1 (3.12) Match the words with pictures 1–5. Then listen and check.

contact lens(es)   grey hair   sideburns   stubble   a tattoo

2 (3.13) Match features 1–11 with these words. Then listen and check.

a beard   dyed hair   eyebrows   eyelashes   a fringe (US: bangs)
a moustache   a parting   a piercing   pierced ears   a scar   wig

3 Which words in 1 and 2 collocate with *get*, *wear* and / or *have*?
You can have sideburns but you can't get or wear them.

4 Make true sentences about yourself. Any similarities?
I've been wearing contact lenses since I was a kid.

3R p.45

Word Bank 14 — Describing objects

1 🔊3.16 Match the materials with photos 1–9. Make a phrase for each with a shared vowel sound. Then listen and check.

Silk pyjamas – both have the sound /i/.

- [ ] alu**min**ium
- [ ] **card**board
- [ ] **cot**ton
- [ ] **leath**er
- [ ] **plas**tic
- [ ] **rub**ber
- [ ] silk
- [ ] steel
- [ ] **wool**(len)

2 In pairs, name something that you a) own and b) use a lot for each material.

> **Tip**
>
> Wood / **wood**en, wool / **wool**len and metal / me**tall**ic have two adjective forms. The shorter ones are much more common. Only use *wooden / woollen / metallic* before a noun.
>
> *A metallic sound   A wooden ship*

3 🔊3.17 Match two words to each picture. Listen and check.

blunt   hard   heavy   light
rough   sharp   smooth   soft

➤ 3E p.40

Word Bank 15 — Describing pictures

1 🔊3.20 Match the phrases with positions 1–9 on the photo. Then listen and check.

- [ ] at the top
- [ ] at the bottom
- [ ] at the front
- [ ] in the bottom left-hand corner
- [ ] in the top right-hand corner
- [ ] in the background
- [ ] in the middle
- [ ] on the left
- [ ] on the right

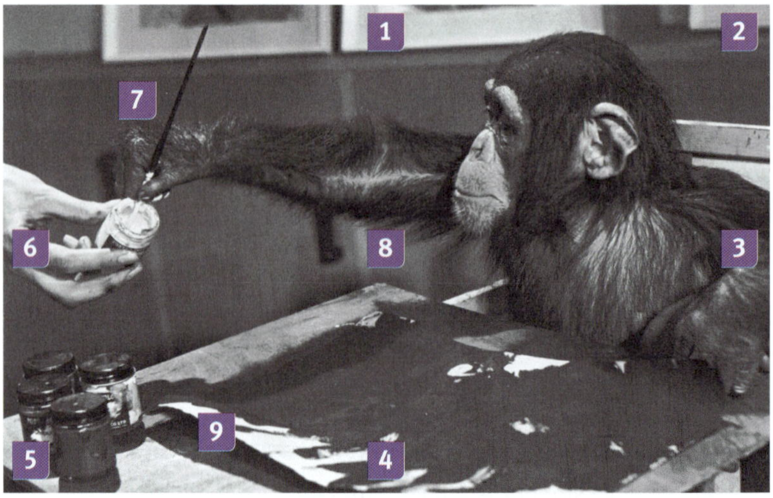

2 In pairs, Ⓐ look back at any picture in this book. Describe it to Ⓑ until Ⓑ remembers the photo or the lesson. Swap roles.

A: *On the left, there's a picture of Barack Obama as a white man. And on the right there's a picture of John McCain as a black man.*
B: *Oh I remember that. It was from an advert. The lesson was about…*

➤ 3F p.42

72

Going to a gig? Word Bank 16

1 4.1 Match the words to the web page, 1–6. Listen and check.

- [ ] encore
- [ ] gig
- [ ] headlining
- [ ] set list
- [ ] support act
- [ ] venue

Chris Ng's Music page!

(1) Concert guide
Green Day in New York!
(2) Green Day
with (3) Kaiser Chiefs
at (4) Madison Square Gardens
The songs they played were amazing! Check it out:
(5) 1. Song of the Century
2. 21st Century Breakdown
3. Know your Enemy
[see all]
And they ended the concert with:
(6) 25. American Idiot
[see all]

2 4.2 Label the photo 7–13:

7 (lead) singer
8 (lead) guitarist
9 drummer
10 bassist
11 on keyboards
12 microphone
13 stage

Listen and check.

3 In pairs, describe the last gig you saw.

I tried to get a ticket to see X's last gig but it was sold out so I saw it on DVD.

4A p.46

UK and US English Word Bank 17

1 4.5 Match the words and pictures. Listen and check. Which form have you heard / used more often? Listen and check. Know any others? Add them in the margin.

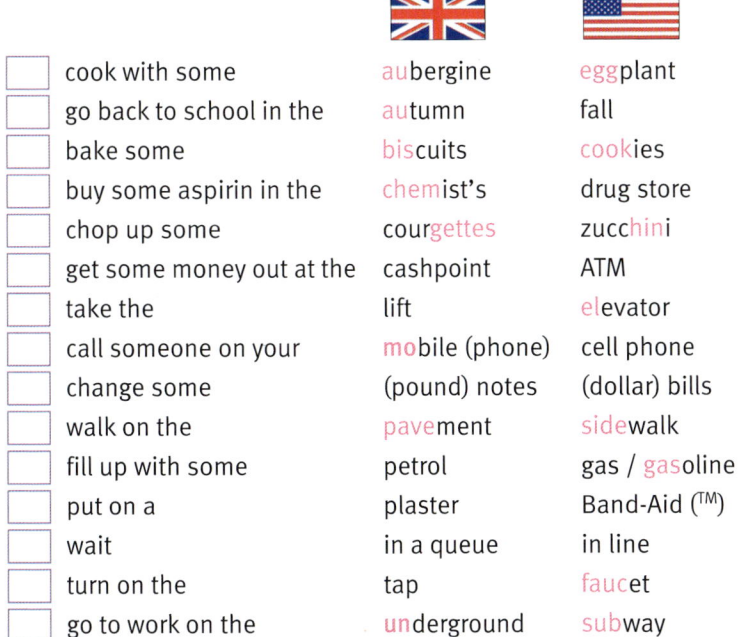

	🇬🇧	🇺🇸
cook with some	aubergine	eggplant
go back to school in the	autumn	fall
bake some	biscuits	cookies
buy some aspirin in the	chemist's	drug store
chop up some	courgettes	zucchini
get some money out at the	cashpoint	ATM
take the	lift	elevator
call someone on your	mobile (phone)	cell phone
change some	(pound) notes	(dollar) bills
walk on the	pavement	sidewalk
fill up with some	petrol	gas / gasoline
put on a	plaster	Band-Aid (™)
wait	in a queue	in line
turn on the	tap	faucet
go to work on the	underground	subway

2 In pairs, test each other. Say the words with the right accent!

How do you say walk on the sidewalk *in British English?*

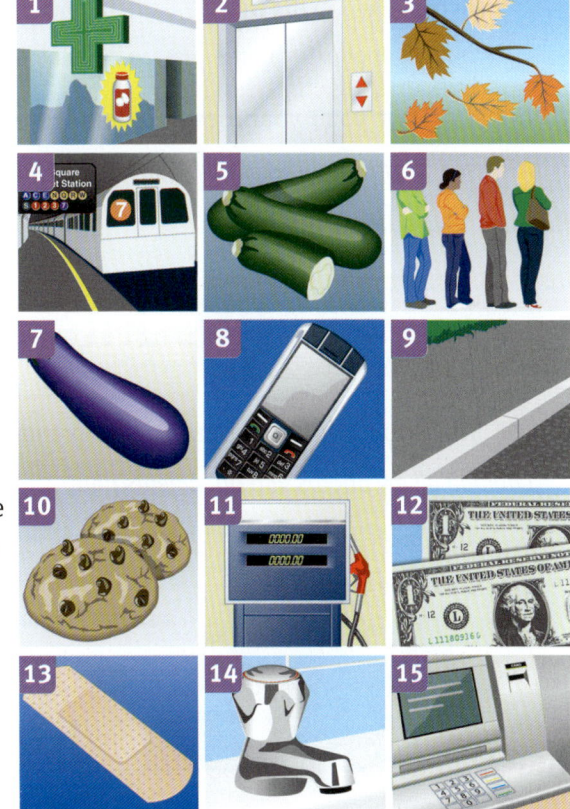

4B p.48

Word Bank 18 — Charity and the environment

1 🔊 4.9 Listen and match the words and pictures 1–6.

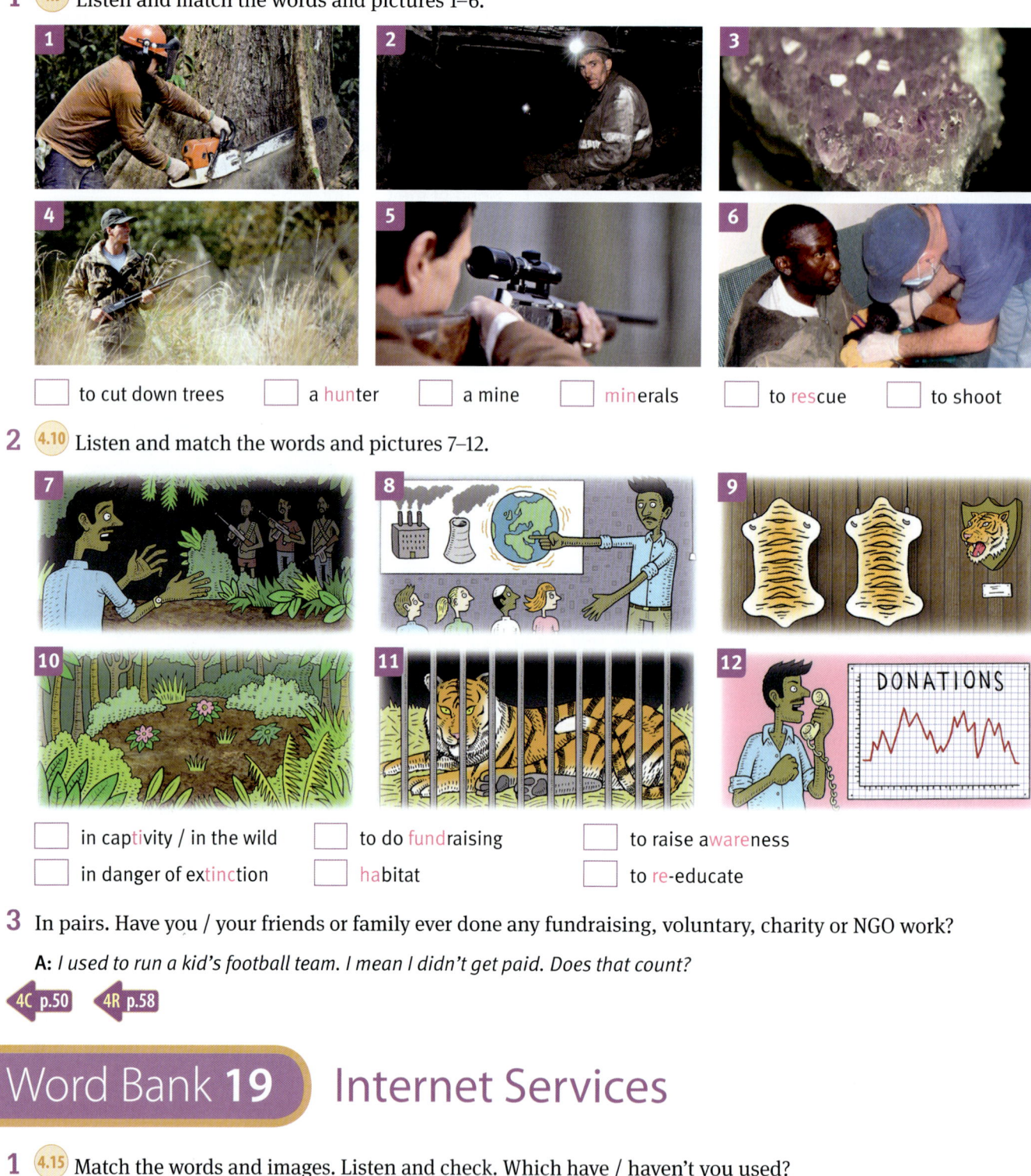

- [ ] to cut down trees
- [ ] a hunter
- [ ] a mine
- [ ] minerals
- [ ] to rescue
- [ ] to shoot

2 🔊 4.10 Listen and match the words and pictures 7–12.

- [ ] in captivity / in the wild
- [ ] to do fundraising
- [ ] to raise awareness
- [ ] in danger of extinction
- [ ] habitat
- [ ] to re-educate

3 In pairs. Have you / your friends or family ever done any fundraising, voluntary, charity or NGO work?

A: *I used to run a kid's football team. I mean I didn't get paid. Does that count?*

▶ 4C p.50 ▶ 4R p.58

Word Bank 19 — Internet Services

1 🔊 4.15 Match the words and images. Listen and check. Which have / haven't you used?

I upload all my photos and documents onto …

- [ ] an e-tailer
- [ ] an online auction
- [ ] an online encyclopedia
- [ ] a search engine
- [ ] a social networking site
- [ ] a video-sharing website
- [ ] a virtual world
- [ ] voice over IP
- [ ] webmail

74

Vowel and consonant sounds — Word Bank 20

20 vowel sounds 1.21 2.25 Listen and chant the 12 vowel sounds.

7 short vowels

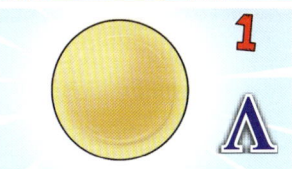

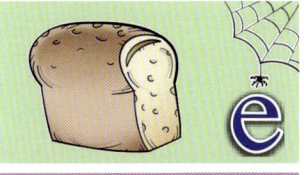

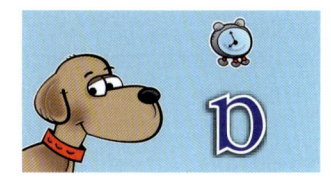

ɪ æ e ɒ
ʌ ʊ ə

5 long vowels

iː ɑː ɜː ɔː uː

1R p.17

8 diphthongs

eɪ aɪ əʊ aʊ
eə ɪə ɔɪ ʊə

2R p.31

24 Consonant sounds 3.25 Listen and chant the 9 (red) unvoiced and 4.21 15 voiced consonants.

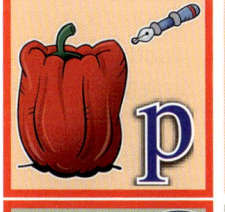

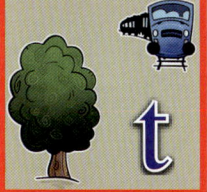

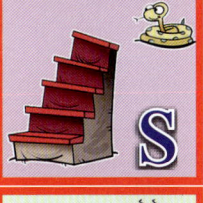

3R p.45

p b k g f v
t d s z ʃ ʒ
θ ð tʃ dʒ h l
r w j m n ŋ

4R p.59

75

Word Bank 21 — Irregular verbs

Infinitive	Past simple	Past participle
be	was / were	been
beat	beat	beat
bet	bet	bet
become	became	become
begin	began	begun
bend	bent	bent
bite	bit	bitten
blow	blew	blown
break	broke	broken
bring	brought	brought
build	built	built
burn	burnt / burned	burnt / burned
buy	bought	bought
can	could	could
catch	caught	caught
choose	chose	chosen
come	came	come
cost	cost	cost
creep	crept	crept
cut	cut	cut
deal	dealt	dealt
do	did	done
draw	drew	drawn
dream	dreamt	dreamt
drink	drank	drunk
drive	drove	driven
eat	ate	eaten
fall	fell	fallen
feed	fed	fed
feel	felt	felt
fight	fought	fought
find	found	found
fly	flew	flown
forget	forgot	forgotten
freeze	froze	frozen
get	got	got / gotten (US)
give	gave	given
go	went	gone
grow	grew	grown
hang	hung	hung
have	had	had
hear	heard	heard
hide	hid	hidden
hit	hit	hit
hold	held	held
hurt	hurt	hurt
keep	kept	kept
know	knew	known
lead	led	led

Infinitive	Past simple	Past participle
learn	learnt / learned	learnt / learned
leave	left	left
lend	lent	lent
let	let	let
lose	lost	lost
make	made	made
mean	meant	meant
meet	met	met
pay	paid	paid
put	put	put
quit	quit	quit
read /ri:d/	read /red/	read /red/
ride	rode	ridden
ring	rang	rung
rise	rose	risen
run	ran	run
say	said	said
see	saw	seen
send	sent	sent
seek	sought	sought
set	set	set
shake	shook	shook
shine	shone	shone
shoot	shot	shot
show	showed	shown
shut	shut	shut
sing	sang	sung
sit	sat	sat
sleep	slept	slept
smell	smelt	smelt
speak	spoke	spoken
spend	spent	spent
spread	spread	spread
stand	stood	stood
steal	stole	stolen
stick	stuck	stuck
sting	stung	stung
swim	swam	swum
take	took	taken
teach	taught	taught
tell	told	told
think	thought	thought
throw	threw	thrown
understand	understood	understood
wake	woke	woken
wear	wore	worn
win	won	won
write	wrote	written

Key: red = only 1 form   blue = 2 different forms   black = 3 different forms

1 (4.22) Listen and chant the 10 verbs in **bold**. Do you think chanting is the best way to learn irregular verbs?

2 Test a partner. A: say two forms (*ride*, *ridden*). B: say the missing one (*rode*).

3 In pairs, group the phrasal verbs, e.g. by similar sounds or spelling. E.g. *grow*, *know*, *throw* — ow / ew / own. how many groups can you make? Which verbs don't fit in any group?

Phrasebook

Unit 1

1 Read the list. Tick ✓ the ones you already use. Look up any you don't know.

- It's always the same. ☐
- It's getting harder and harder to… ☐
- I've had enough. ☐
- It's a waste of time. ☐
- That doesn't count. ☐
- I can't put up with it any more. ☐
- Mind you, I wasn't surprised ☐
- I'm fed up with it! ☐
- What's the hurry? ☐
- It's amazing how… ☐
- And another thing… ☐
- It happens all the time. ☐
- Great to hear from you! ☐
- Stay put. ☐
- What a pain! ☐
- Good for her! ☐
- It's got me thinking. ☐
- Let's get going! ☐
- Anything in particular? ☐
- It wouldn't hurt to… ☐
- You'll love it! ☐

More formal

- It was a relief when… ☐
- As far as I was concerned… ☐
- It was difficult at first. ☐
- There are (some) advantages ☐

2 (P.1) Listen and repeat, copying the speed, stress, links and intonation. Try to start using the ones you haven't ticked.

Unit 2

1 Double-check you now know, and can use, all the phrases in Unit 1.

2 Read the list. Tick ✓ the ones you already use. Look up any you don't know.

- Let's just say (that)… ☐
- That's very common. ☐
- No, not at all. ☐
- In the end… ☐
- To be honest… ☐
- By accident ☐
- It's clear to see (that)… ☐
- I bet it was! ☐
- We'll need to keep an eye on… ☐
- I'll have to try that out. ☐
- It's a mystery to me. ☐
- I'm a big fan. ☐
- Give me a call. ☐
- See you then! ☐
- Once in a while… ☐
- Trust me. ☐
- Tell me more. ☐
- The moral of the story is… ☐
- I'm fairly sure about… ☐
- I could do with one of those. ☐
- How come…? ☐
- Good for you. ☐
- You're joking! ☐
- That's life. ☐

More formal

- I am writing to inform you… ☐
- I comfort myself with the thought that… ☐
- The first thing to say is that… ☐

3 (P.2) Listen and repeat, copying the speed, stress, links and intonation. Try to start using the ones you haven't ticked.

77

Phrasebook

Unit 3

1. Double-check you now know and can use all the phrases in Unit 2.

2. Read the list. Tick ✓ the ones you already use. Look up any you don't know.

- You're‿a real star ☐
- For my money… ☐
- Thank you for putting me‿up. ☐
- I'll just go‿and get… ☐
- He'll get‿over‿it. ☐
- How‿is‿it that…? ☐
- I think‿I'm coming down with something. ☐
- I'm‿off to work. ☐
- I don't feel‿at‿all well. ☐
- I suppose so. ☐
- I'm ready for‿anything. ☐
- Tell me about it! ☐
- I'm sick‿of it. ☐
- I've never known‿anything like‿it! ☐
- Enough‿is‿enough. ☐
- The thing‿is… ☐
- You could‿always… ☐
- Don't make the mistake‿of… ☐
- Get you! You're so clever! ☐
- Come to think‿of‿it… ☐
- We're supposed to be … ☐
- It's‿a nightmare. ☐
- It'll‿only take a minute. ☐
- I can't figure‿out how to… ☐
- I've told you how to do this‿a million times. ☐
- What's that supposed to mean? ☐
- I'll see what‿I can do. ☐
- Here we‿are now… ☐
- There we go. ☐

More formal

- By contrast… ☐
- In‿effect… ☐
- I have to say, I think… ☐

3. [P.3] Listen and repeat, copying the speed, stress, links and intonation. Try to start using the ones you haven't ticked.

Unit 4

1. Double-check you now know and can use all the phrases in Unit 3.

2. Read the list. Tick ✓ the ones you already use. Look up any you don't know.

- You're not going to believe this but… ☐
- (It was my brother), you see. ☐
- A complete disaster ☐
- A scary moment ☐
- All night long ☐
- There's plenty of fish in the sea. ☐
- That was it. ☐
- Luckily, nothing happened. ☐
- It was ten times better. ☐
- Forget‿it! ☐
- What would‿I do without…? ☐
- It happens to us‿all. ☐
- We'll see what happens. ☐
- I got hooked. ☐
- I had‿a lot‿of fun. ☐
- It was wonderful. ☐
- I can't help‿it! ☐
- That's how‿I started‿out ☐
- Imagine that. ☐
- It did the complete opposite. ☐
- I ran‿into Suzie‿in the lift. ☐
- …so to speak. ☐
- All right, I confess! ☐
- I've changed my mind. ☐
- I know‿all‿about that… ☐
- Go‿on, try one. ☐
- What rubbish! ☐
- That's‿all we have time for. ☐
- Don't get me wrong. ☐
- One thing‿I'm sure‿of is… ☐
- That's‿all I have to say. ☐
- There's plenty‿of fish‿in the sea. ☐

More formal

- The fear remains that… ☐
- I'm‿ashamed to say. ☐
- One thing‿I would say‿is that… ☐
- On the one hand… On the‿other hand. ☐
- My initial feelings were… ☐

3. [P.4] Listen and repeat, copying the speed, stress, links and intonation. Try to start using the ones you haven't ticked.

4. Look back and check you've ticked and can now use all the phrases in Phrasebook 1–4.

Life crisis! 1A

Vocabulary

Word Bank 1: Collocations p. 64

Nouns: concept, corporation, debt, employee, gadgets, grade, independence, loans, living, luxury, media, qualifications, secretary, suffering
Verbs: afford, earn   **Prepositions:** within   **Adjectives:** affordable, depressing, mindless, proper
Expressions: to coin (a phrase), for ages, for free, difficult at first, twenty-somethings

1 Complete the verb forms. Use contractions.

1 Stefania _____ me yesterday she _____ had 16 interviews but not one job offer.
2 Günter isn't _____ _____ come to school today so you _____ have to teach his classes this afternoon.
3 I _____ believe that you _____ really applying for jobs. You never _____ anything!
4 Iris _____ tired all day yesterday because she _____ _____ looking at jobs on the Net till 3 a.m.
5 _____ you seen that new TV show that everyone's _____ talking about in the papers?

2 (1.1) Listen and number the verbs in the order you hear them 1–8.

a ☐ come _____
b ☐ finish _____
c ☐ hold _____
d ☐ mean _____
e ☐ read _____
f ☒ 1 see _____
g ☐ study _____
h ☐ work _____

3 Listen again. Write the correct form of each verb in ex 2.

4 (1.2) Listen to a father and daughter. True (T) or false (F)?

1 Shirine hasn't been looking for work yet. ☐
2 Her dad works in the insurance industry. ☐
3 Her degree course took three years. ☐
4 She has money worries so she needs a job now. ☐
5 Her dad thinks doing work experience is a waste of time. ☐
6 Some big fashion houses have contacted her. ☐
7 Shirley's friend Valentina is enjoying her job. ☐

5 Correct these typical collocation mistakes. Listen again to check.

1 The summer's almost ~~complete~~... *over*
2 You could walk direct into a job there.
3 I'm not heavy in debt or anything.
4 ...to make work experience in a fashion house.
5 I've already applied to every job I've seen...
6 I've sent over my CV to all the fashion houses.
7 You'll be under a lot of stressful.
8 She's already sick to dead of it.

UNIT 1   79

1B Happy families?

Vocabulary

Word Bank 2: Phrasal verbs p. 65
Nouns: growth, in-laws, nerves, policy, predictions, quest, siblings, spectrum, sink, struggle, survey, nails
Verbs: (go) grey, juggle, introduce, lead, mark, restrict, submit
Adjectives: formal, full-time, urban, unforeseen   **Expressions:** hanging around, three-part, right next door

1 Match sentences 1–4 with cartoons A–D.

1 "Do you think the neighbours have fallen out?"
2 "Kids grow up so fast these days."
3 "He takes after his father."
4 "Hang on – if you're moving out, I'll come with you!"

2 Complete with the phrasal verbs.

| break up | fall out | get on |
| live up | move out | tell off |

1 A Why has Tim _____ _____ with his sister? They're hardly talking to each other.
   B It's because she's always _____ him _____ for being untidy, for being noisy in the house. He's sick to death of it.

2 A Do you _____ _____ well with your sister?
   B Yeah, we're really good friends. I mean, I _____ _____ of my parents' house about two years ago, but we still talk every day on the phone.

3 A Why do you think Anja and Frank _____ _____ last month? It's sad that they're not together any more.
   B He's very relaxed and she was very ambitious so I think he didn't _____ _____ to her expectations.

3 Match the phrasal verbs in 1–8 with patterns a–d.

a separable PVs   c intransitive PVs
b inseparable PVs   d three-part PVs

1 I'm really **looking forward to** seeing my new granddaughter.
2 I **came across** a really interesting article when I was reading the paper yesterday.
3 Can you **turn** the computer **on** because the kids want to use the Net?
4 We're visiting your grandparents today so **put** that nice top **on** that they gave you.
5 We know a really good babysitter who always **looks after** the kids when we go out.
6 Your cousin's **staying over** tomorrow so we need to clean the house.
7 Our school parties are always the same. We need to **come up with** something different.
8 Whenever we get calls trying to sell us something, my mum just **hangs up**.

4 Match the phrasal verbs in 3 with definitions a–h.

a start wearing
b spend the night in someone else's house
c feel happy about a future event
d think of a new idea
e find by chance
f care for, be responsible for
g stop using the telephone
h start a machine

5 (1.3) Underline the main stress in each bold phrasal verb. Listen, check and complete.

1 We were **going out** together _____ almost a year before we got married. I was really **looking forward to** _____ his wife, but to be honest, married life was a bit _____. It didn't **live up** _____ my expectations.

2 I was very happy when I was **growing up**. I've got three brothers and I've always **got on** really well with them. They did **take after** my dad a little more though, because they loved cars and things, which never really interested me.

3 I was always **falling out** with my sister, because she was always borrowing my things without asking. My mum used to **tell** her **off** too but she never listened. To be honest, it was a relief when she finally **moved out**.

Life since Web 2.0

Vocabulary

Word Bank 3: Words for feelings p.66
Nouns: canoe, dishwasher, mountaineers, narrative, shame, users
Verbs: go canoeing, celebrate, emphasise, be fed up, moan, slave away, wander (a)round
Adjectives: hilarious, keenest, key, previous, typical, unlocked   **Adverbs:** beforehand, obviously
Expressions: to go out (with someone), (it) went wrong, it was (my) fault, to go red, luckily, it gets worse...

1 Complete the puzzle. What's the word in grey?

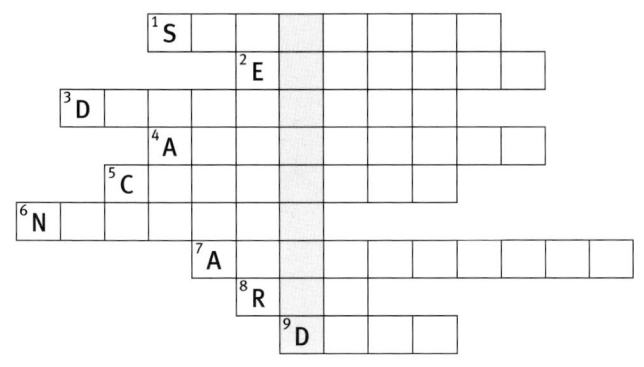

1. S
2. E
3. D
4. A
5. C
6. N
7. A
8. R
9. D

1 Lots of work and no time to relax, so you feel... out.
2 Very happy and enthusiastic, eg, before a big match.
3 Really pleased about something, e.g. good news.
4 Absolutely terrible.
5 If you don't understand something, you feel...
6 Worried, for example, before a big exam.
7 Very, very surprised.
8 When you're embarrassed, you go this colour.
9 Another way to say sad or depressed.

2 (1.4) Listen and match the dialogues with a–f.

a shocked   d nervous
b go red   e down
c exhausted   f delighted

3 Complete with the verb in the correct tense.

1 I was going to put the pictures on the website but when I went online, I saw that Keiko __had done__ it already. *(do)* (3)
2 I _____ a shower so I didn't hear the phone. *(have)* (2)
3 We took loads of photos while we _____ *(stay)* in Beijing. (2)
4 When we got back to our towels, someone _____ our bags! *(steal)* (1)
5 We had to eat out because it was a national holiday and all the shops were closed. Helmut _____ to go to the supermarket the day before. *(forget)* (11)
6 Anita missed her stop because she _____ loads of messages on her mobile. *(send)* (1)

4 (1.5) Underline all the syllables and words in ex 3 that are pronounced /ə/. The number of /ə/s in each sentence is given in brackets. Listen and check.

5 Circle the correct option in the news article.

Melissa Brandts and her husband Jackson had [1]*hiked / been hiking* in the mountains of Canada when they decided to take a quick photo for their family album. They [2]*just set / had just set* the timer and sat down together, when a local squirrel who had [3]*watched / been watching* them, suddenly jumped in front of the camera. While the Brandts [4]*were still laughing / had still laughed*, the squirrel was caught dead centre.

Melissa and Jackson then [5]*put / had put* their picture online, where it immediately became an Internet sensation. Soon afterwards, some people claimed that the photo [6]*had been faked / was being faked* because it seemed too good to be true. However Mrs Brandt insists that the photo is real. Various experts have also agreed that it is genuine. A photo that [7]*had been created / was being created* on a computer could never have the same quality of hair against water. This was 100% real: a shot in a million.

A curious ground squirrel has brought plenty of attention to the Brandts.

Photograph by: Melissa Brandts, National Geographic Stock, Calgary Herald

1D Trading places

Vocabulary

Word Bank 4: Intensifiers p.66
Nouns: bullet, chef, expedition, metro, trams, Western (film), workplace, X-rays   **Verbs:** consist of, scan
Adjectives: awesome, boiling, equivalent, Finnish, fizzy, impressed, solid, spicy, starving, tough, uncommon
Other: herself, clearly, literally, ridiculously, unbelievably
Expressions: in the beginning, to be honest, from time to time, 24/7, trading places

1 Cross out the option which doesn't work.

1 The test was *completely / extremely / unbelievably* difficult.
2 I don't understand what I have to do. I'm *absolutely / completely / totally* confused.
3 Everything in the shop was *incredibly / ridiculously / totally* old.
4 The special effects in the film were *absolutely / extremely / totally* amazing!
5 It's *absolutely / completely / unbelievably* certain that we're not going to win the competition.
6 Thank you for looking after my grandmother. That was *extremely / incredibly / absolutely* kind of you.

2 (1.6) Listen to five people talking about living abroad. Choose the best answers.

1 The man most likes the Slovenian
 a scenery. b architecture.
 c opportunities for winter sports.
2 Pablo's unhappy because he
 a hates the food in New York.
 b doesn't like living in the big city.
 c isn't enjoying his job.
3 Marc likes the Icelandic
 a weather. b wildlife. c clothes shops.
4 The woman will get tickets to the game
 a from someone outside the stadium.
 b from a relative.
 c because she's a member of a special organisation.
5 When Danny got lost in Seoul, he was looking for
 a the underground. b the city centre.
 c his language school.

3 (1.7) Match the bold words to their pronunciation a–f. Use the chart on page 75 to help you. Listen and check.

a /red/ b /rəʊ/ c /juːzd/ d /raʊ/ e /juːst/ f /riːd/

1 We **used** to live in Vietnam. ☐
2 Sorry, I've **used** all the milk. ☐
3 Have you **read** the paper yet? ☐
4 I **read** your blog every day. I love it. ☐
5 We're already in the cinema, in the back **row**. ☐
6 Jo's having a huge **row** with Mika. She's really angry. ☐

4 Circle the correct option.

Marta Hi Luis. How's it going? Are you enjoying university life?
Luis Hi Marta. Well, I'm slowly ¹*getting / being* used to it. I mean the courses are OK, because I'm used to ²*sit / sitting* in classes all day.
Marta But...?
Luis It's my flat. I'm sharing with six other people and I just can't ³*be / get* used to it.
Marta Why? Isn't it fun sharing a house? I ⁴*was used to / used to* love living in my shared house when I was at college.
Luis Really? Well, I ⁵*am / get* used to living somewhere very clean, but this house is really dirty.
Marta Are you living with girls or boys?
Luis Six boys.
Marta Hmm.
Luis And another thing, I can't ⁶*be / get* used to all the visitors. There're always new people in the house – friends of friends, sleeping on the sofa and things like that.
Marta You know, I think you'll just have to ⁷*be / get* used to that.
Luis Yeah? It's going to be a long year.
Marta It certainly is!

Study tip

Record new words in a phrase or a sentence. A personal example from your own life is most useful.
I used to have *incredibly* long hair but it's much shorter now.
Also look for synonyms and antonyms (opposites) of new words. Your dictionary or an online thesaurus can help you do this.

The grass is always greener

Vocabulary

Word Bank 1: Collocations p.64
Nouns: actor, colleague, delay, grandma, madwoman, malaria, pain, Shakespeare, side, suitcase, visa
Verbs: freeze, pour
Adjectives: earning, greener, influential, present, realistic, thirty
Expressions: What a pain. I'm fed up. I'll fix it for you.

1 Complete the blog with these words.

to meet   near him   a drink
thinking   a cold   younger

Last year we were invited to see the film premier of *The Curious Case of Benjamin Button*. It's the story of a person who is born as a ninety-year-old man and then gets ¹_____ until he becomes a baby. It was a great day out even though my brother got ²_____ so he had to stay in bed and he wasn't able to come. I was hoping that I would get ³_____ Brad Pitt and all the other actors. But of course there were so many people there that I couldn't get ⁴_____ . But when I went to get ⁵_____ after the performance, I did see the film's director and I was able to take his photo, which was amazing. Anyway, the film itself was really good and it really got me ⁶_____ about aging and what it means to us in our lives. I'd recommend anyone to watch it.

2 Correct the sentences. One has no mistake.

1 Silke has gone to see the doctor because she's got a flu.
2 The amount of crime in this city is getting worst all the time.
3 All this bad news has got me worry about the future.
4 I don't know if we'll get close to any lions while we're on safari.
5 We really want to get know you better.
6 I'm really hungry. Shall we become a pizza?

3 Circle the correct verb form.

Hi Dagmara

Great to hear from you! Everything's fine here too – really nice and sunny here in Almaty. If you were here, ¹*you'd be / you were* on the beach every day! We're having loads of parties too and I've been taking loads of pictures. If you go on Facebook, ²*you see / you'll see* them all on my page. There are some really cool ones!

Anyway, sorry to hear that you're not having such a good time in the UK. It sounds like it's pretty difficult to meet people. If I ³*were / would be* you, I'd try to do a language exchange or something. That's a good way to meet people. I ⁴*won't come / wouldn't* come home now though – you've paid a lot of money for your course so you should complete it. And anyway, you won't be on your own all summer. Jake told me that if he ⁵*has / had* time, he'll come and see you in London, so that's some good news, isn't it? It's always fun being in a foreign country if you ⁶*get / would get* lots of visitors from home.

Anyway, gotta go and teach! The other students miss you. If ⁷*you want / you'll want* to talk, I'll be online all day tomorrow, so send me a message and we can chat online.

Speak soon!
LOL
Gemma

4 (1.8) Listen. True (T) or false (F)?

1 Tara's reading the newspaper.
2 Tara's seen a job in the Arctic.
3 Chen's unenthusiastic about the job.
4 The job would take about twelve weeks.
5 Tara's currently a student.
6 The magazine's extremely popular.
7 At the end of the conversation, Tara and Chen agree.

5 Write the missing words. Listen again and check.

1 If you / it, you / /. (read, see).
2 If we / an interesting job, we / to apply for it straightaway.
3 If I / that job, I would / / chance to do something really exciting.
4 If I / in your shoes, I /n't / think of doing this.
5 If I stay here, I/ never get the job I /.
6 If I / apply for the job and they accepted /, I / have professional articles published by that organisation.
7 If you / online now, I'll show / their website and that / change your opinion.

6 Are 1–7 in ex 5 the zero (Z), first (F), or second (S) conditional?

1F Going away

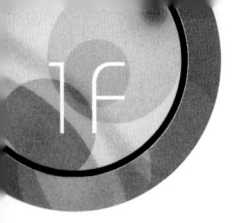

Vocabulary

Word Bank 2: Phrasal verbs p.65
Nouns: Acropolis, Athens, beach, Brazil, buildings, coach, cuisine, delicacies, ferry(ies), guidebooks, impressions, island, itinerary, locals, massage, museums
Verbs: go backpacking, calculate, connect
Adjectives: adventurous, careful, cautious, classic, east, north, south, urban, west
Prepositions: furthest   **Expressions:** fire away!, first impressions, show (someone) the sights,

Test yourself on Unit 1

1 Do these exercises to check your progress.

2 Count your **correct** answers.
Write the total number in the box.
Total: ☐ /40 correct answers

3 Try to understand your mistakes. If necessary,
- read the **Essential Grammar**, and/or
- look at the Student Book lesson again, or
- ask your teacher.

4 How do you feel about this unit? Tick (✓) a box.

---

1 Match the sentence halves.

1 Liam had a huge row with his girlfriend and now he's broken   [f]
2 The visitors were late so we were hanging ☐
3 There's no sun cream. We've completely run ☐
4 The trip was supposed to be secret but Ella found ☐
5 I'm sure he's going to turn ☐
6 It's a real crisis. We don't have enough money to get ☐

a out about it.
b by.
c around for hours.
d up late.
e out of it.
f up with her.

2 Tick ✓ or correct the sentences.

1 I bought some rice and fish because ~~I'll make~~ *I'm going to make* a paella.
2 I can't come to tomorrow's meeting as I'll fly to Miami. ☐
3 They'll speak to you sometime next week. ☐
4 We'll go on a walking holiday next month that I booked online. ☐
5 I go to a party after work tonight. Do you want to come too? ☐
6 It'll be really sunny at the weekend. ☐

I can use all the main tenses appropriately. **Lesson 1A**

3 Complete with the correct tense.

1 I ___met___ Mehmet when I was working in Turkey. *(meet)*
2 After I read the email, I _____ it. *(delete)*
3 I _____ in ghosts. *(not / believe)*
4 Chou _____ here since April. He finishes in September. *(study)*
5 The shop always _____ at 9 am. *(open)*
6 I'm tired. I think I _____ to bed. *(go)*
7 Joe! Help me! I can't answer the phone because I _____ the ironing. *(do)*

I can use phrasal verbs correctly. **Lesson 1B**

4 Put the particle in the correct place.

1 Carmen's just started a new school and she's finding it a bit difficult to fit *in*. *(in)*
2 My parents were disappointed in me but I couldn't live to their high expectations. *(up)*
3 Ruben doesn't get well with his boss. *(on)*
4 Ludmilla really takes her mother. They look almost identical! *(after)*
5 After my parents divorced, I was brought by my uncle and aunt. *(up)*
6 Have you heard that Min is going with Roger? *(out)*
7 My mum really told me after I failed all my exams. *(off)*

84

I can narrate a story. Lesson 1C

5 Circle the correct option in the story.

One night I ¹*lay / was lying* in bed when I heard a strange noise outside my window. I was really surprised because I live in an apartment on the second floor. Anyway, I opened the curtains, and I ²*saw / had seen* my neighbour at the window. He was in his pyjamas and his eyes were open. He ³*had stood / was standing* halfway up a ladder that some workman had left next to the house. They ⁴*had repaired / had been repairing* the roof all week and the work still wasn't finished. Anyway, I opened the window and I brought my neighbour inside. He woke up then but didn't remember anything! I realised then that he ⁵*had sleepwalked / had been sleepwalking* and that he ⁶*hadn't known / hadn't been knowing* that he was out in the street in his pyjamas in the middle of the night! Lucky for him he didn't hurt himself!

I can talk about habits, old and new. Lesson 1D

6 Complete with *used to*, *be used to*, or *get used to* + the verbs in brackets.

1 Nowadays, I _____ (hear) lots of noise at night, but when I moved to the city, I couldn't sleep.

2 Agenta hates her new job. It starts at 11 p.m. and she can't _____ (work) at nights.

3 We _____ (not / watch) much TV as children because we were always playing outside.

4 He _____ (not / use) a Mac because he always used a PC before.

5 The kids got really sick on the sailing holiday because they _____ (not be) on a boat.

6 _____ you _____ (go) to school with me back in the 1990s?

I can talk about realistic and hypothetical possibilities. Lesson 1E

7 Complete the sentence using the correct form of the words.

1 _____ he'll love this book.
if / Luca / like / science fiction

2 _____ I wouldn't do that course.
if / I / be / you

3 If all our customers ate meat, _____ we / not / put / vegetarian option on the menu

4 _____ you get sunburn.
if / you / not / put on / suncream

5 If you give me your email address, _____ I / send / you / the photos

6 If I met the president of the USA, _____ . (I / talk / him / global warming)

I can use a wide range of new vocabulary in English. Lessons 1A–1F

8 Can you remember...

1 **WB** Collocations (p.64):
9 job search collocations?

2 **WB** Phrasal verbs (p.65):
Which of the 19 are separable?

3 **WB** Words for feelings (p.66):
Can you pronounce the 12 words for feelings correctly?

4 **WB** Intensifiers (p.66):
7 different intensifiers?

5 Phrasebook 1 (p.77):
Can you use and pronounce well all 25 phrases?

6 All the new vocabulary from Lessons 1A–1E?

UNIT 1 85

2A The first job I ever had was …

Vocabulary

Word Bank 5: Adjective suffixes p.67
Nouns: carbon, coal, developments, dust, factory, fields, impact, industry, loaf, machine, petrol, photocopying, prevention, rubber, ruler, skin, soap, stapler, tyres
Verbs: complain, distribute, operate, get rid of, wash
Adjectives: artificial, automatic, comfortable, covered, deserted, endless, excellent, folding, forgotten, imaginative, noteworthy, outdoors, promotional, ruined, touched, tough, weekly
Prepositions: afterwards   **Other:** basically   **Expressions:** let's just say… , I bet it was!

1 Complete the puzzle with adjectives from Word Bank 5p. 67. What's the word in grey?

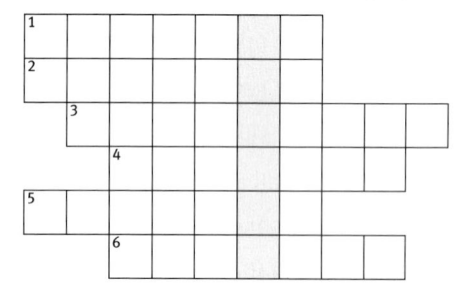

1 Extremely angry.
2 Something that continues and never seems to stop.
3 Something that could hurt or kill you.
4 When you only think of yourself.
5 When you do everything you can to prevent accidents, etc…
6 Something so terrible that it is almost impossible to live with.

2 (2.1) Listen to six conversations about Marco Jordan. Are they positive (+) or negative (-) about him?

1 ☐   2 ☐   3 ☐   4 ☐   5 ☐   6 ☐

3 Listen again and order the adjectives 1–6 as you hear them.

a ☐ unforgettable   d ☐ flexible
b ☐ environmental   e ☐ responsible
c ☐ trustworthy   f ☐ professional

4 Circle the correct option.

1 Go to the office *which / where* is on the second floor.
2 The explanation, *why / which* was on the website, was completely unbelievable.
3 Miss Cozzi, *who / that* taught us Italian last year, is going to teach all our lessons next year.
4 Is that the café *which / where* you met Jo?
5 There's a holiday on September 11th *when / which* is only celebrated in this part of the country.
6 Jukka, *who's / whose* birthday is tomorrow, is the oldest student in the class.

5 Mark the relative clauses in 4 defining (D) or non-defining (N).

6 Complete the relative clauses with one word in each gap.

NTZ – No Take Zone

Everyone knows that the sea is in danger from over-fishing. Thankfully, there are a number of people [1]_____ are working to protect the marine environment. One such group is an organisation called COAST, [2]_____ main role is to protect the sea around the Scottish island of Arran. On the east side of the island, they have created an NTZ, [3]_____ means 'No Take Zone'. This is a part of the sea [4]_____ nobody is allowed to take fish. The reason [5]_____ they placed the NTZ there is that it is an area where many fish, lobsters and other shellfish lay eggs. In 2003, [6]_____ the NTZ was founded, few could have imagined what a success it was going to be, but now the number of animals in the sea around Arran is increasing all the time.

White lies

2B

Vocabulary

Word Bank 6: Negative prefixes p.68
Nouns: agreement, comment, discounts, experiment, forehead, hamster, honesty, liar, liver, nightclub, onions, organisations, permission, pet, phone-in, subconscious, vet
Adjectives: basic, facial, false, reluctant, spot, touching, underage, unwilling   **Adverbs:** confidently
Expressions: I left in the end, from all over the world, that's unfair, anything else?

1 Complete the adjectives in these emails.

a The fish was completely in _ _ _ _ _ _. It tasted like a piece of wet cardboard.

b I don't care if you are moving offices. That's totally ir_ _ _ _ _ _ _ _! You promised to deliver the posters next Monday, and that's when I want them!

c He's always downloading films for free from the Internet. Like most people his age, he doesn't seem to think it's il_ _ _ _ _.

d There were twenty steps and no lifts! How are dis _ _ _ _ _ people like me supposed to get in to see the exhibition?

e We asked the class to submit handwritten essays, but we couldn't read half of them because they were almost il_ _ _ _ _ _ _.

f I am writing to inform your readers about the terrible and im_ _ _ _ _ treatment of workers on farms in this country.

g Raj goes crazy as soon as he gets on the road. He's so im_ _ _ _ _ _ and I'm sure that he's going to cause an accident one day.

h He wanted me to sign a contract which contained information which wasn't true. I refused of course, but he just laughed when I told him it was dis_ _ _ _ _ _.

i People from the city come here to go walking in the country and they're always letting their dogs scare the cows or forgetting to close the gates. Honestly, how can people be so ir_ _ _ _ _ _ _ _ _ _?

j Don't ask her immediately if she wants to go out with you. Be a bit more in_ _ _ _ _ _ so she guesses what you're going to do. Then it won't be a surprise.

2 Match texts a–j in ex 1 to 1–10.

1 ☐ someone complaining about the entrance to a museum
2 ☐ somebody criticizing a lawyer
3 ☐ a parent worrying about what her son is doing
4 ☐ a friend giving relationship advice
5 ☐ a teacher complaining about her students
6 ☐ a customer complaining about poor service
7 ☐ an elderly lady complaining about tourists
8 ☐ a wife complaining about her husband
9 ☐ a restaurant customer complaining
10 ☐ an email to a newspaper

3 Complete the conversation with question tags. D = detective, PO = police officer.

D This isn't the scene of the crime, [1]_____?

PO Yes, sir. It happened right here.

D So, earlier today Mrs Lee was walking through the zoo when she was robbed. She didn't see the robbers, [2]_____?

PO No, sir.

D And she'd been there for about an hour, [3]_____?

PO That's correct.

D And then someone hit her on the head.

PO She was hit from behind. If she'd been hit from the front, she'd have seen her attackers, [4]_____?

D But nothing valuable was taken, [5]_____?

PO No. the thieves escaped with a wig, her false teeth, umbrella, and sandwiches.

D She still has her money, credit cards, [6]_____?

PO That's right. The thieves didn't take any of that.

D I think I'm going to have to speak to her again, [7]_____?

PO You don't think she's lying, [8]_____?

D Well, we shouldn't reject any possibilities yet, [9]_____? Oh, I wish those monkeys would keep quiet!

PO Yes, I don't know why they're so noisy today!

4 (2.2) Listen and check your answers. Notice the intonation in the question tags.

Unit 2   87

2C Dress-down Friday

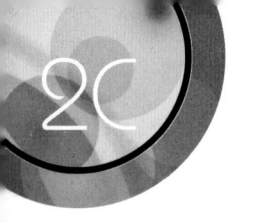

Vocabulary

Word Bank 7: Reporting verbs p.68

Nouns: casino, catwalk, comfort, debut, desk, dress code, editor, exposure, formalwear, gimmicks, glossary, influence, interpretation, laughter, preconceptions, pride, reaction, sea, shelves, shoppers, shorts, side, socks, standards, stranger, suit, shorts, terms

Verbs: approach, bare (teeth), escape, praise, require, store, suit, tidy

Adjectives: absent, alternative, casual, compulsory, convenient, dress-down, emerging, grateful, inappropriate, knee-length, predictable, required, spicy, staple, unfortunate

Adverbs: casually, personally, rapidly, simply

1 Complete the jokes with two of the reporting verbs.

  a informs   replies   says

  A man goes to the doctor and puts his arm behind his head. He _____ "doctor, it hurts when I do this."
  The doctor _____ "Well, don't do it, then."

  b asked   pointed out   told

  John Lennon was sitting at home when a beetle came in through the window. After flying around for a bit, the beetle _____ John, "Help! How do I get out of this room?"
  John looked at the beetle and _____ it "Hey little beetle, I'll help you out. You know, my band was named after you."
  "What?" The beetle replied. "You've got a band called 'Steve'?"

  c complains   explains   informs

  A customer is eating dinner in a restaurant when she calls the waiter over and _____ that there's a fly in her soup.
  The waiter inspects the soup and then calmly _____ the customer, "Don't say it too loudly, madam, or everyone'll want one."

  d explains   mentions   tells

  A man starts his own company and he opens a new office. As soon as his first visitor arrives, he picks up the phone and pretends to chat to a customer. He _____ all the money that he's making and how successful his company is. Finally, he finishes the call and says to his visitor "I'm very sorry about that. How can I help you?"
  "I'm here to connect your new phone…" the visitor _____.

2 Put these sentences from ex 1 into reported speech.

  1 "Don't do it, then."
    The doctor _____

  2 "My band was named after you."
    John Lennon _____

  3 "Everyone will want one."
    The waiter _____

  4 "I'm here to connect your new phone…"
    The man _____

3 Correct two typical mistakes in each sentence.

  1 They asked to me what did I wear to the party.
    <u>They asked me what I wore to the party.</u>

  2 He pointed me out that dress-down Friday fun.
    _____

  3 They asked me weather could they wear shorts.
    _____

  4 The boss told to everyone wear smart casual clothes.
    _____

  5 Isidore said me to don't wear trainers to the office.
    _____

4 (2.3) Listen. Write the messages in reported speech.

  1 Nana said _____.
  2 Mum asked _____.
  3 Sergio said _____.
  4 Ahmed asked _____.

5 Who used these phrases? Listen again and check.

> Call me.   Give me a call.
> I hope to see you here.   See you then!

88

Cash on the side

Vocabulary

Word Bank 8: Money p.69
Nouns: advertising, contract, fee, fraction, payment, salary, subscription, tragedy
Verbs: babysit, drive around, pay out, promote, top up
Adjectives: brand, economic, identical, mystery   Adverbs: rarely
Expressions: the credit crunch, for half the price, on the side

1 Complete the puzzle. What's the word in grey?

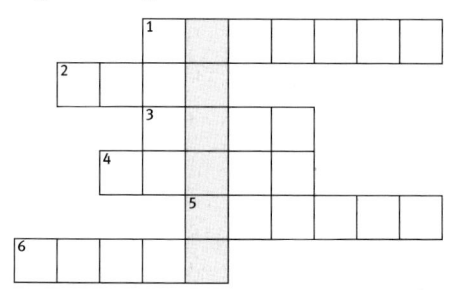

1 Unless you're well-off, you often have to _____ your belt.
2 A plumber often gets paid cash in _____.
3 I'm a teacher but I drive a taxi at the weekend to make money on the _____.
4 I don't have any cash. I'm completely _____.
5 Those bankers are _____ serious money.
6 I do all the work, but because we're on a team, everyone else _____ a cut of profits too.

2 (2.4) Listen to four conversations. Are they in a good ☺ or bad ☹ financial situation?

1 ☺ ☹   3 ☺ ☹
2 ☺ ☹   4 ☺ ☹

3 Complete the sentences. Listen again to check.

1 It's amazing. You're _____ to be making some _____ money here.
2 Yesterday you _____ me you were _____. And now you have this. Another new computer game! How on earth _____ you afford it?
3 Now look, your father and I are _____ some problems and we _____ need to tighten our _____.
4 You'll be able _____ take a _____ of the profits, and we get paid _____ in hand.

Study tip

The first time you do a workbook exercise, write your answers on a separate paper. Then, some time later (e.g. after a week or so) do the exercises again. See how much better your answers are the second time around. Which mistakes (if any) do you repeat?

4 Circle the correct option in the autobiography.

Mila Gutierrez

When she was a teenager, no one thought Mila was going to be a success. But after she after left school, she went on ¹*becoming / to become* a successful journalist. She'd always wanted ²*writing / to write* for the newspapers, so, as soon as she left school she tried ³*getting / to get* some work experience. She got hundreds of rejection letters but she kept ⁴*sending / to send* out her CV, until finally she got a position. On the job, she followed another reporter around, and he taught her everything she needed ⁵*knowing / to know*. Although they weren't paying her, she went on ⁶*working / to work* for them because she was learning so much. It was a really difficult time as she couldn't afford ⁷*paying / to pay* her rent or anything – she was dependent on her parent's support. But she never regretted ⁸*taking / to take* the job, because now she's working for a national magazine.

5 Correct ten typical mistakes in the story.

When I was a student, I always wanted going out every night with my friends, but I couldn't always afford joining them. One day, I remember to ask some friends if they knew of any job offers. Stupidly, I told them that I didn't mind to do anything. Almost immediately, my friend Katja asked me if I enjoyed to paint and art and I said 'yeah'. The next day one of her friends sent me an email and asked me to be a model for her drawing class. Because I was in a hurry, I didn't stop reading everything but I did remember to ask her how much she was paying me. She told me €30 for one hour's work! I said 'yes'.

That afternoon I went to the gallery. The room was full of old ladies who were talking very loudly. But when I came in, everyone stopped to talk and stared. The art teacher said 'Hello, you can take your clothes off over there.'

"Er, don't you mean my coat?" I replied.

"No, your clothes," she said and walked off.

Well, I suppose I could have gone home but I stayed. I'll never forget to sit in that chair, in nothing at all, while very elderly ladies silently drew my body. At the end of the class, I just took the money and ran. I learned my lesson. When someone offers you a job, don't forget asking exactly what they want you to do.

Unit 2 89

2E The shape of things to come

Vocabulary

Word Bank 9: Noun forms p.69
Nouns: alternatives, carton, enthusiasm, global warming, lobby, percentage, reserves, species, transplant
Verbs: double, revolutionise   Adjectives: advanced, allergic, dramatic, drastic, renewable, robotic
Expressions: Hurry up!

1 Do the crossword.

ACROSS

3 Buying pirate DVDs is a _____. You've got to stop doing it!

6 The murderer was sent to _____ for 35 years.

DOWN

1 After I broke my leg, I had to have an operation and I was in _____ for over five hours.

2 Personally, I'm a bit of an _____. I reckon the future's going to be pretty good.

4 I don't really like my gas oven. I preferred my old _____ one.

5 I'm a bit of a _____. I think people only came to listen to these politicians because there's free food and drinks!

2 Complete with the correct form of the words in CAPITAL letters.

1 A: The _surgeons_ have been operating on the patient for almost an hour.   SURGERY
   B: Don't worry. They are _____ that the operation will be a complete success.   OPTIMIST

2 A: I'm reading a biography of a man who was wrongly _____ for twenty years for robbery.   PRISON
   B: You mean he wasn't really a _____ at all! That's terrible.   CRIME

3 A: The kids don't really want to go on the school trip. They only seem _____ because they get a day off school.   ENTHUSIASM
   B: Don't be so _____. I think some of the kids really enjoy going to museums.   CYNICISM

3 Choose the correct option.

1 It's 4 pm so right now, Mike will just *arrive / be arriving* in Tashkent.

2 By 2050, everyone will *believe / be believing* in global warming.

3 Don't come before 7 pm because I won't *have had / be having* enough time to prepare dinner.

4 When you get to the station, you'll recognise me because I'll *have worn / be wearing* a red scarf.

5 We have to go to the mechanic's tomorrow as it *won't be open / have opened* on Sunday.

4 (2.5) Listen to a robotics expert, Radek Cerny. (T) True or (F) False?

1 Radek thinks people are already using robots a lot.

2 He thinks we won't need to drive cars in future.

3 According to Radek, it will never be possible to create machines with feelings.

4 The interviewer thinks her husband is a bad driver.

5 Radek thinks that he won't be alive in 2050.

6 In 2050, there'll be 1,000,000,000 people over the age of 65.

7 In the future, many robots will be working in domestic situations.

8 He's very concerned about improving human health.

5 (2.6) Try to remember these sentences. Each ✻ = one missing word. Listen again to check and repeat. Stress the parts of words in CAPITALS.

1 So, ✻, robots ✻ become a BIGger part ✻ ✻ LIVES.

2 I believe that ✻ ✻ FUTure, EVerybody will ✻ a PASSenger because cars will ✻ driving themSELVES.

3 And ✻ inCREDibly, ✻ about 2050, the EXperts ✻ ✻ developed maCHINES with eMOtions.

4 So not ONLY ✻ the cars ✻ driving ✻ AROUND but they ✻ ALso be TERRified of CRAShing or ✻ an ACCident.

5 In 2050, there will be ALMOST ✻ BILLion people ✻ the age of 65. This ✻ that MANY ✻ the nEW developments in robotics, will ✻ ✻ inVENted for OLDer PEople.

Testing times

Vocabulary

Word Bank 9: Noun forms p.69
Nouns: ambulance, the emergency services, examiner, gate, patient, track
Verbs: jump, reverse, smash into   **Adjectives:** determined, hopeless, mere, satellite
Adverbs: illegally   **Expressions:** en route, get into trouble, How come, How sweet!

Test yourself on Unit 2

1. Do these exercises to check your progress.
2. Count your **correct** answers. Write the total number in the box.
   Total: ☐ /40 correct answers
3. Try to understand your mistakes. If necessary,
   - read the **Essential Grammar**, and / or
   - look at the Student Book lesson again, or
   - ask your teacher.
4. How do you feel about this unit? Tick (✓) a box.

1 Complete the car words puzzle. What's the word in grey?

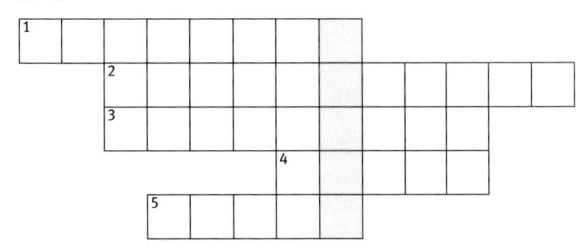

1. You hold the _____ wheel with your hands and use it to move the car.
2. Put your foot on the _____ to make the car go faster.
3. Use the _____ to show other drivers that you are turning left or right.
4. Put your foot on the _____ slow the car down or to stop.
5. The _____ are the rubber part of the wheel.

I can describe past possibilities. Lesson 2F

2 Complete with the most appropriate modal verb (+ or –).

1. It's raining. I knew I _____ have bought an umbrella.
2. I can't find my pen. I suppose I _____ have left it in the office.
3. I _____ have come to school on my bike because my brother's borrowed it.
4. Peter told Susie that her ex-boyfriend is getting married! She's furious. Personally, I _____ have told her anything.
5. Eulalia's car isn't here so she _____ have gone home.

I can describe and define things. Lesson 2A

3 Tick ✓ or correct the sentences.

1. Do you know who's sweater this is?
2. I'm looking for the house which Shakespeare was born.
3. We took this photo on the day which there was that enormous thunderstorm.
4. Now I know the reason why Xavier and Olga have been arguing.
5. There's the man that we spoke to yesterday.
6. We are looking after several animals who mothers were killed by hunters.

Unit 2   91

2F

I can ask and check using question tags. *Lesson 2B*

4 Complete with the right question tag.

1 You speak French, ___don't you___?
2 I'm meeting you tomorrow, _____?
3 Joe'd like to watch the film with us, _____?
4 The police won't want to speak to me, _____?
5 You spoke to Eric before he went home, _____?
6 Herbert's going to call everyone later, _____?
7 We'd never met Waris before, _____?

I can report speech. *Lesson 2C*

5 Report what people said to you.

1 Dave: We don't have enough money to go to Cuba.
   Dave pointed out that we didn't have enough money to go to Cuba
2 The doctor: "Don't go to work again until next week."
   He told _____
3 The teacher: "Have you finished your project?"
   The teacher asked _____
4 Ursula: "What time does the film start?"
   She asked _____
5 Dad: "I'll meet you here at four o'clock."
   Dad said _____
6 Abdul: "Did you see the email that I sent yesterday?"
   Abdul asked _____
7 Your sister: "You can't do this exercise like that."
   My sister explained _____

I can combine verbs correctly. *Lesson 2D*

6 Complete with the correct forms.

1 We don't mind _____ for you. *(wait)*
2 Don't forget _____ the clothes out of the washing machine before you go to bed. *(take)*
3 I remember _____ to the lakes with you and your parents. An amazing day. *(go)*
4 Nobody enjoys _____ homework at the weekend. *(do)*
5 When we reach the top of the mountain, we'll stop _____ a break. *(have)*
6 I can't afford _____ a new computer! *(buy)*

I can make predictions using three forms of will. *Lesson 2E*

7 Circle the correct option.

1 Don't phone Daniela. She won't *get / have got* home yet.
2 You can't give this exercise to the students. They won't *understand / be understanding* it.
3 Sorry, Reuben's not here. He'll probably *have / be having* his coffee break.
4 I can relax on Friday because I'll *be finishing / have finished* all my work by then.
5 Ladies and gentlemen, due to bad turbulence, we'll *be arriving / have arrived* a little later than we'd expected.
6 I'll *do / have done* the washing up after I have a cup of tea. Just wait a couple of minutes.

I can use a wide range of new vocabulary in English. *Lessons 2A–2F*

8 Can you remember…

1 **WB** Adjective suffixes (p.67)
   2 words for each adjective suffix?
2 **WB** Negative prefixes (p.68)
   all the negative prefixes?
3 **WB** Reporting verbs (p.68)
   the 16 reporting verbs?
4 **WB** Money idioms (p.69)
   the 6 money idioms?
5 **WB** Noun forms (p.69)
   all the adjectives and the nouns?
6 **Phrasebook 2** (p.77)
   Can you remember and use all 27 phrases?
7 All the new vocabulary from Lessons 2A–2E?

I am what I am

Vocabulary

Nouns: attitude, campaign, covergirl, debate, institution, manipulation, opponent, poster, retouching, the shoot, sleeves
Verbs: desire, doctor, put someone up, shave
Adjectives: adored, African-American, excessive, presidential, slim   **Adverbs:** currently
Expressions: for my money, on the part of, Tell me a little about yourself

1 (3.1) Listen to four conversations about changes to image. In which conversation ...

- do they talk about a famous person? ☐
- is someone wearing unusual clothes? ☐
- are people at work? ☐
- are the people shopping? ☐

2 Complete with *a / an*, *the* or Ø (zero article). Then listen again and check.

A Maria Well, how about [1]_____ top like this? Oh yes, that's really you!
  Al [2]_____ yellow one? I don't think I could wear that. It's [3]_____ bit bright.

B Becky His advisors told him he needs to change his look to appeal to [4]_____ young people. I don't think it's working. I mean, look at his hair!
  George And why's he wearing [5]_____ track suit? That's [6]_____ stupidest thing I've ever seen!

C Katya But I mean... look what you're wearing! You know we're not allowed to wear [7]_____ jeans to [8]_____ work!
  Joe It's OK. We're only giving them [9]_____ information. They're not buying anything from us.

D Vera Do you want be [10]_____ model, then?
  Paula Yeah! That's why I'm dressed up like this. This is what all [11]_____ trendy people are wearing in London and New York at the moment.

3 Circle the one which doesn't need *the*.

1 Ukraine, United Arab Emirates, USA, (Uruguay)
2 North Pole, Antarctic, Asia, Equator
3 Everest, Andes, Himalayas, Matterhorn
4 White House, Sheraton Hotel, Buckingham Palace, Kremlin
5 Mekong River, Lake Titicaca, Caribbean, Pacific Ocean
6 Underground, Oxford Street, Museum of Modern Art, Mona Lisa

Study tip

Knowing when to use or omit 'the' isn't easy. When you learn a new rule, try to think of other examples. E.g. *Road names don't take 'the' – except the High Street!* Looking out for exceptions helps you to remember the rule. If you're not sure, google the word and look at the examples.

4 Circle the correct options (Ø = no article).

In 2001, director Wes Anderson released [1]*The / Ø* Royal Tanenbaums, a film about a fictional family of overachievers. The mother is [2]*a / the* famous author and all three children have become famous in their professions (business, tennis and working in the theatre). [3]*Ø / The* film looks at the lives of [4]*the / Ø* famous families in general and how this affects the children. It is also very, very funny with [5]*the / a* wonderful performance from Gene Hackman in a starring role as the father.

However, interestingly, many of the actors have [6]*the / Ø* famous parents in real life. Anjelica Huston, who plays the family's mother, is [7]*a / the* member of one of [8]*Ø / the* most successful families in Hollywood. She, her father, and her grandfather have all won Oscars in their careers. The younger members of the cast also have [9]*a / the* family connection. Two characters are played by real-life brothers, Owen and Luke Wilson. It's [10]*a / Ø* real case of life imitating art.

UNIT 3   93

3B Man-flu

Vocabulary

Word Bank 11: Illnesses p.70

Nouns: appointment, aspirin, blanket, bout, caffeine, central heating, conflict, harmony, hormone, life expectancy, muscle, oestrogen, portion, risk, stereotyping, testosterone, victim, warning

Verbs: blame, bring (something) down, come down, get over (something), insist, play out, retreat, seek, suffer, whimper

Adjectives: academic, aware, outdated, painful, scientific, sub-tropical, sympathetic, violent

Adverbs: definitely, dramatically, likely, noisily   **Expressions:** after all, a ripe old age, the last minute

1 Cross out the silent letters in these words.

> climb   doubt   exhausted   foreigner
> honest   island   parliament   psychiatrist
> salmon   soften   vehicle   Wednesday

2 Cross out the odd word out.

1 I'm looking for Mrs Diana Wu. I believe she's a *hypochondriac / nurse / patient* in this hospital.
2 Mike's in bed with a *cold / fever / sniff*.
3 I need to take a paracetamol because I've got a *cough / headache / sore throat*.
4 If you feel *sick / sneeze / stiff*, you shouldn't play football this afternoon.
5 The doctor came round and told me the kids have *flu / a high temperature / patient*.
6 Most people have the same symptoms: they'll *cough / sneeze / sore throat* all the time.

3 **3.2** Listen and match six people to their illnesses. There is one extra.

a ☐ a high temperature   e ☐ sniffing a lot
b ☐ a stiff back   f ☐ a cough
c ☐ a sore throat   g ☐ a headache
d ☐ sneezing a lot

4 Correct two typical mistakes with articles in each sentence.

1 I'm not feeling a too good. I think I've got the a cold.
2 I'm going to chemist's to get something for sore throat.
3 As soon as I got up in morning I felt the shoulder was really stiff.
4 One of best ways to avoid catching a flu is to wash your hands regularly.
5 According to thermometer, you have the high temperature.
6 Every patients has a same symptoms, so they're probably suffering from same illness.

5 Rewrite as indirect questions, using the words in bold.

1 Can I help you with anything?   **would / you**
_____

2 Can I check my emails on your laptop?   **do / mind**
_____

3 Do you want to eat out with us tomorrow night? **wondering / if**
_____

4 Does Julio have a driving license?   **know / whether**
_____

5 Can you look after my dog for a few minutes? **would / mind**
_____

6 Are you free to come round and fix my computer tomorrow night?   **could / you**
_____

6 **3.3** Listen once and answer.

1 How many students are in class today?
2 Where are the rest?

7 Listen again and count the direct questions you hear.

8 Listen once more and shadow-read **3.3** on p 110. Make the links, copy the sentence stress and the intonation on the direct questions.

The art of the street

Vocabulary

Word Bank 12: Word + preposition p.71
Nouns: bronze, busker, case, compatriot, fame, installation, lookalike, sculptor, shades, statue, violinist, volume
Verbs: imitate, immortalise, pedal, stick out of, survey **Adjectives:** unsure
Adverbs: currently, furiously, honestly, interestingly
Expressions: enough is enough, I'm sick of it!, in disguise, to drive someone mad

1 Complete the vowels in the words.

1. As the p_ _nt_r of m_st_rp_ _c_s like the Mona Lisa, Leonardo da Vinci was the greatest _rt_st of his time.
2. There's a very strange _nst_ll_t_ _n in the modern _rt g_ll_ry. It's in the shape of a man but made from dirty knives and forks. They call it a sc_lpt_r_ too, but I think it's just a mess.
3. As a sc_lpt_r, Michelangelo's most famous w_rk was the st_t_ _ of David, which is now in Florence. He carved it from a single block of m_rbl_.
4. Although the German Albrecht Dürer was a m_ster of p_ _nt_ng in o_ls, he is most r_n_wn_d today for his dr_w_ng of two hands.

2 (3.4) Listen and match conversations 1–3 to the cartoons.

A   B

C

3 Add two words to each sentence. Listen again to check.

a. Do you want to my new sculpture? I've made it of wood.
b. It's statue a cow.
c. Ah, it's work of a conceptual.
d. It's a made out of. It's an installation.
e. Have you seen Timmy's paintings? This has colours: red, yellow and white.
f. No. But I have seen drawings – over the walls downstairs!

4 Complete with present perfect verb forms, one simple, the other continuous. Use contractions.

1. I'm just writing to say how much I enjoyed your recent exhibition. I _____ galleries for over thirty years, and I don't think I _____ such a fantastic exhibition. (*visit, see*)

2. I am writing to complain about your company. We _____ for a parcel to be delivered for over three weeks and it still _____. How long is this situation going to continue? (*wait, not arrive*)

3. I _____ your office four times to ask Mr Jackson for an interview but every time I call, I'm told he's busy. We _____ to arrange an interview with him for over a year now, and we'd very much like to hear if he's interested in talking to us. (*phone, try*)

4. The situation is impossible! The builders _____ in the building next door for over a month now and the noise they make is unbelievable! The noise _____ me _____ every day at 7.30 am for the past week and I'm sick to death of it! (*work, wake up*)

5. I am just writing to mention a new discovery. I _____ from asthma all my life and for people in my situation it's something that can make our lives very difficult. However, recently I _____ a new medicine and it really relieves my asthma symptoms. It's absolutely wonderful! (*suffer, take*)

5 Tick ✓ the sentences where both options are correct.

1. ☐ I've *been looking / looked* for that book all over town.
2. ☐ They've *won / been winning* two gold medals in total.
3. ☐ We've *been living / lived* in this apartment for years.
4. ☐ Mr Soneji has *taught / been teaching* the same class all year.
5. ☐ Your eyes are sore because you've *worked / been working* on the computer.

3D Changing times

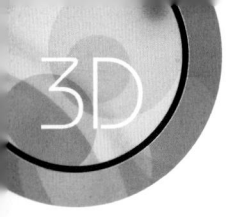

Vocabulary

Word Bank 13: The face and appearance p.71
Nouns: make up, manicure, mascara, moisturiser, polo shirt, saxophone, razor, wrinkles
Verbs: dye, fade, smooth   **Adjectives:** checked, exotic   **Adverbs:** gently, upstairs
Expressions: to cost the earth, Get you!, vice-versa

1 Read the sentences. What is **it** / **they**?

1 It's a picture that is drawn on the body. They're usually permanent. _tattoo_
2 It's the hair above your eyes. _____
3 It's a piece of metal (e.g. like an earring) that you insert into your skin for decoration. _____
4 **They**'re the hair around your eyes (women put mascara on them). _____
5 It's a hairstyle where the hair is cut in a straight line across the forehead. _____
6 If a man doesn't shave for two or three days, he gets **it** on his chin before he gets a beard. _____
7 **They** are worn by lots of people instead of glasses. _____
8 It's a hairstyle where you have a line in the middle of your hair, and you move some hair to the left and some hair to the right. _____

2 (3.5) Listen and match conversations 1–4 to photos A–D.

A ☐   B ☐   C ☐   D ☐

3 (3.6) Underline the stressed words (the number is given in brackets) and add the linking sounds. Listen to check.

1 I wish I'd got them years ago. (2)
2 If only I'd listened to her. I wanted a piercing too. (3)
3 Honestly, I wish you'd shave more often! (3)
4 I love your fringe. And your long dark hair. If only I had hair like that (3)

Study tip

Only stress pronouns for special emphasis, eg as in 2 and 4 above, to contrast I with someone else.

4 Which sentences in ex 3 are talking about:
a the present? _____   b the past? _____

5 Complete with the words in brackets.

1 The job interview was a disaster! I wish I _____ there! (never / go)
2 If only I _____ Timo that I saw Erica with another guy in that café. They've broken up because of me. (not / tell)
3 If only you _____ a bit harder! Then you wouldn't have all these problems at school! (work)
4 I wish I _____ on that link. That's the reason why I've got this virus on my PC! (click)
5 I wish you _____ me before you invite all these visitors round. I never know who I'm going to find in the house when I come home. (ask)
6 I'd only answered half the questions when the test ended. If only I _____ more time! I could have got a much better mark. (have)

6 Express the same meaning, using **wish** or **if only**. Use contractions.

1 I should have left earlier. I was twenty minutes late!
  If only I _'d left earlier_ .
2 You ought to listen to my advice.
  If only _____
3 I can't believe I posted that picture on the Internet.
  I wish _____
4 Living in this town is so boring!
  I wish _____
5 I can't do the course because I don't speak very good Spanish.
  If only _____
6 Why don't you tell me before you invite people round?
  I wish _____

Gadget mania!

Vocabulary

Word Bank 14: Describing objects p.72

Nouns: beak, button, cap, cone, invention, kettle, monitor, mug, namesake, penguin, sensation, tail, tongue, typewriter, USB port, wires   **Verbs:** attach, dip, download, enable, lift, turn around
Adjectives: cutting-edge, handy, latex, reptilian, telepathic   **Adverbs:** automatically
Expressions: to cost €15 a time, on special offer

1 Circle ten materials in the snake. Which one isn't both a noun and an adjective?

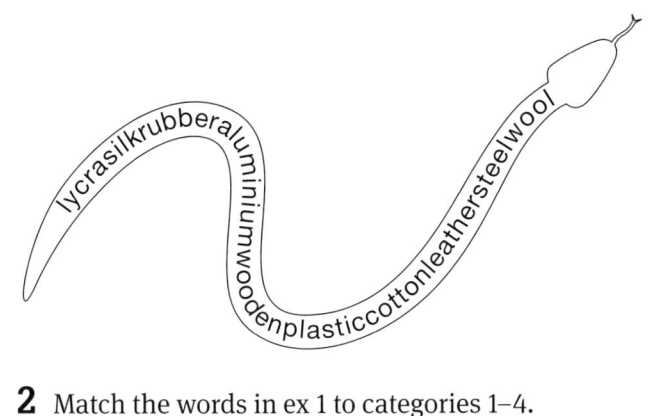

lycrasilkrubberaluminiumwoodenplasticcottonleathersteelwool

2 Match the words in ex 1 to categories 1–4.

  1 Three materials that come from animals
   _____   _____   _____

  2 Two metals   _____   _____

  3 Three products from plants or trees. Which is from plants?
   _____   _____   _____

  4 Three artificial materials invented by scientists
   _____   _____   _____

3 (3.7) Listen to six conversations. Who's going…

  a cycling? ☐   d walking in the countryside? ☐
  b to a wedding? ☐ e to the recycling bins? ☐
  c to work? ☐   f to a children's party? ☐

4 Listen again and underline the stressed words (the number is given in brackets). Use script (3.7) on p. 111 to check your answers. Shadow read, link and copy the intonation.

  1 That's a good idea. (1)
  2 Oh, stop complaining. Put on your rubber boots and let's go. (3)
  3 All right, all right. There's no need to shout. (1)
  4 Oh, I like your lycra shorts. (2)
  5 Look at this. We're all wearing these pink silk dresses. They're beautiful. (2)
  6 Why don't you take them out more often, then? (1)

5 Circle the correct options in the biography.

Isaac Newton (1642–1727)

If an apple ¹*didn't fall / hadn't fallen* on Isaac Newton's head one day in 1666, the whole history of the world ²*will be / would have been* different. After watching the apple fall, Newton discovered gravity. Soon afterwards, he was considered one of the great men of the new scientific age. But if people ³*had known / would have known* more about Newton, they ⁴*had discovered / would have discovered* that he was not just a scientist. Newton was also obsessed with alchemy: the idea that a special substance ('the philosopher's stone') could change ordinary metals into gold! If he ⁵*found / had found* it, he ⁶*would have become / will have become* unbelievably rich. Of course, the philosopher's stone was just a legend, but Newton really believed in it. If his notes on alchemy ⁷*hadn't been destroyed / hadn't destroyed* in a fire in the 1670s, hundreds of papers ⁸*are surviving / would have survived* to show that he spent years and years searching for something that had never existed.

6 Complete these third conditionals.

  1 The play was awful. If I _____ in the audience, I would have left and gone home. *(be)*
  2 B! If you'd worked harder, you _____ an A! *(get)*
  3 If you _____ a ticket like everybody else, the police wouldn't have taken it away. *(buy)*
  4 It _____ a lot more if we hadn't booked online. *(cost)*
  5 It wouldn't have damaged the furniture, if you _____ it on its own. *(not / leave)*

7 Match the sentences in ex 6 with speakers a–e.

  a somebody who's car has been removed ☐
  b somebody talking about a badly behaved dog ☐
  c a theatre director criticising his own production ☐
  d a parent who's unimpressed with exam results ☐
  e somebody talking about arranging seats at a concert ☐

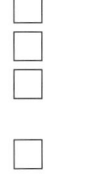

Unit 3   97

3F Artist at work!

Vocabulary

Word Bank 15: Describing pictures p.72
Nouns: chimpanzee, cover, exhibition, gorilla, memory stick, orang-utan, reward, skateboard, surface
Verbs: feed, log on, spread, sting, toss
Adjectives: rare
Adverbs: rather

Test yourself on Unit 3

1. Do these exercises to check your progress.
2. Count your **correct** answers. Write the total number in the box.
   Total: ☐ /40 correct answers
3. Try to understand your mistakes. If necessary,
   - read the **Essential Grammar**, and / or
   - look at the Student Book lesson again, or
   - ask your teacher.
4. How do you feel about this unit? Tick (✓) a box.

---

1 Circle the correct option in the description. Label the sketch a–e.

My favourite picture is a photo that my dad took when we were on a family holiday in Switzerland. It's really funny because ¹*in / on* the middle of the picture, my brother is falling into a lake! We were on a boat and our dog, Skipper, had just jumped out. You can see his head ²*at / in* the bottom left-hand corner. My brother went after him and fell in the water! ³*In / On* the left of the picture, you can see my mum – she looks really angry! ⁴*At / On* the bottom of the picture there's another boat with my uncle in, and he's shouting something too. It's a really funny picture, and I know the date exactly too, because ⁵*at / on* the top of the photo someone has written May 12th, 1999.

2 Complete with the past participles of these verbs. There's one extra.

| bite | draw | dream | feed | freeze | spread | sting |

1 Last night, I _dreamt_ I was a child again.
2 The monkey's _____ the paint all over the paper.
3 I've _____ a picture of the house.
4 She's been _____ by a bee.
5 The water's completely _____.
6 The animals were _____ a mixture of fruit and nuts.

I can use articles accurately. **Lesson 3A**

3 Tick ✓ or correct the sentences.

1 The shoe shop in *the* High Street
2 They've sent this letter to the wrong address. The Jacksons live next door.
3 It was the first time that I'd seen Adriatic Sea.
4 My dad works as firefighter.
5 Usain Bolt is the faster man in the world.
6 I hate sausages. I never eat them.
7 Disabled should have the same career opportunities as everybody else.

98

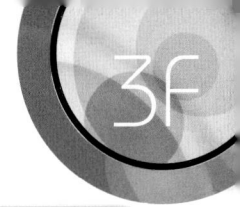

I can use indirect questions. Lesson 3B

4 Add one missing word to each sentence.

1 _Could_ you help me carry this bag?
2 I was wondering you could help me.
3 Would mind waiting outside for a minute?
4 Do you know if Giovanni coming to the class today?
5 Do you mind lunch later today?
6 Would you like me take the children to school today?
7 Could take these rubbish bags outside?

I can describe recent activities. Lesson 3C

5 Circle the correct option.

1 Come and look outside! It's *snowed / been snowing*.
2 I don't think we've *met / been meeting*. I'm Arkady.
3 She's *painted / been painting* that picture for years and it's still not finished.
4 Ania's got a cold so she's already *gone / been going* to bed.
5 I love *Star Wars*. I've *seen / been seeing* it about a hundred times!
6 Rick won't get off the phone. He's *talked / been talking* for ages!

I can express wishes and regrets. Lesson 3D

6 Complete with the verbs.

1 Niko's left for Florida. I wish _____ time to say goodbye to him. *(have)*
2 If only I _____ my last job. I've been unemployed for months. *(not / quit)*
3 I always get so embarrassed. If only I _____ red every time I stand in front of a group! *(not / go)*
4 I wish you _____ talking when I'm trying to watch the TV! *(stop)*
5 I should never have complained about the teacher to Julie. If only I _____ he was her father! *(know)*
6 I wish I _____ my watch off before I went in the swimming pool. It's completely broken now. *(take)*

I can express hypothesise about the past. Lesson 3E

7 Complete this chain story.

1 If my alarm clock had rung I would have got up on time.
2 If .... I wouldn't have missed the bus.
3 If .... I would have arrived at work on time.
4 If I .... I wouldn't have upset my boss.
5 If I .... I wouldn't have lost my job.
6 I wish my ....

I can use a wide range of new vocabulary in English. Lessons 3A–3F

8 Can you remember...

1 **WB** Illnesses (p.70)
   3 diseases and 6 symptoms?
2 **WB** Word + preposition (p.71)
   12 words + preposition collocations??
3 **WB** The face and appearance (p.71)
   Can you pronounce the 16 words correctly?
4 **WB** Describing objects (p.72)
   9 words for materials?
5 **WB** Describing pictures (p.72)
   9 different positions in a picture?
6 **Phrasebook 3** (p.78)
   Can you use and pronounce well all 32 phrases?
7 All the new vocabulary from Lessons 3A–3E?

Unit 3   99

4A Live: tonight!

Vocabulary

Word Bank 16: Going to a gig? p.73
Nouns: album, camel, festival, gig, highlight, performance, setting
Verbs: blow, crash into, rise   Adjectives: exact, hazardous, theatrical, tragic
Expressions: in the heart of

1 Complete the crossword with concert words.

ACROSS
2 A band stands on this so the audience can see them.
4 Nowadays, most bands make much more money when they _____ on tour than they do from selling CDs.
6 At the end of a show, bands usually come back to do an _____ of one or two more songs.
7 The order of songs at a concert is called a set _____.

DOWN
1 A building or a location where musical events take place.
2 A band that appears before the main singer is called the _____ act.
3 An informal word for a concert, especially a rock concert.
5 Pavarotti once sang _____ to half a million people Central Park, NY.

2 Complete with the correct form of these words. There are two extra.

atmosphere   come   encore   gig   headline   performer
play   set   stage   support act   venue

Hi Katie!

How are you doing? I had to write 'cos last week your favourite band ¹_____ here in Mexico City! Yeah, Radiohead finally came back and this time I didn't miss them!! ☺ The ²_____ for the gig was the Foro Sol stadium, where we saw Madonna last year. But it was ten times better.

Lucia came too tho she doesn't really like them – she wanted to see the ³_____, Kraftwerk. They were an old German electronic band from the 70s but she loves them for some reason. We were a bit late getting in and when we finally did, the ⁴_____ had already started ☹, but we still got to hear all their best stuff.

Then we had to wait a bit for Radiohead. The ⁵_____ was amazing: people were shouting and singing their songs. When they finally came on ⁶_____ – it was awesome. We'd managed to get right up to the front! Thom Yorke is an amazing ⁷_____ live, and I just loved his singing. They played all my favourites like 'Climbing up the walls': there must have been about 20 songs in the ⁸_____. And afterwards, they came back on and did two ⁹_____. The last song was 'Creep': you would have died! When they went off, I cried it was that good.

Anyway, hope you're not too jealous! He, he.

Skype soon
Paco

3 Express similar ideas using the future in the past. Use contractions where possible.

1 It'll be sunny all weekend.
   I thought it'd be sunny so I didn't take an umbrella.
2 The venue's going to be the baseball stadium.
   According to the newspaper, _____, but in the end it was the city park.
3 The coach to the concert is leaving at 2 p.m.
   We had to hurry because _____.
4 REM are headlining the event.
   I read online that _____ but it was just a rumour.
5 Our kids will be standing right by the stage.
   I was sure that _____.
6 The metro is to stay open late so people can get home after the gig.
   Apparently, _____. But it was so crowded it was impossible to get on.

4 🔊 4.1 Listen twice to five conversations and identify….

1 the name of the support band and if they were good.
2 why they made a mistake and why they got wet.
3 two things the speaker liked about Robbie Williams.
4 the biggest problem at the concert.
5 the best bit of the concert.

5 Go to audioscript 4.1 p. 111 to check. Listen, shadow read, mark the links and copy the intonation.

How technology can change your life

4B

Vocabulary

Word Bank 17: UK and US English p.73
Nouns: brunette, courage, dilemma, intern, journal, recipe, reunion
Verbs: bake, build up, get off
Adjectives: obsessed
Adverbs: non-stop, nowadays, seriously
Expressions: love at first sight

1 Write the British equivalent of the American words. How do you say the word in grey in US English?

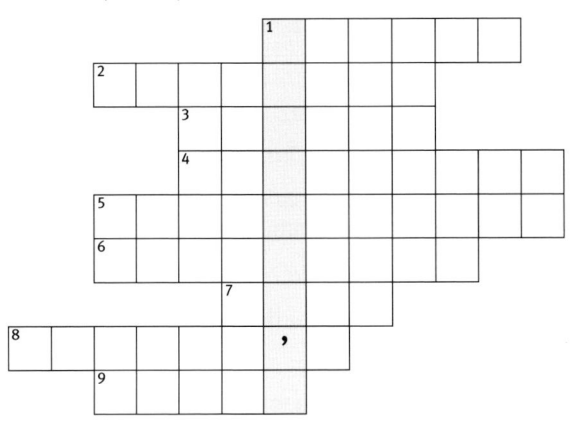

1 Fall (the season, not the verb)
2 Cookies
3 Cell phone
4 Drug store
5 Subway
6 Zucchini
7 Elevator
8 Sidewalk
9 A line (of people)

2 (4.2) Correct the mistake in 1–6. Listen and check.

1 Don't worry, though, my office is only few floors up.
2 We've only got a bit cough medicine left.
3 When she put her photo on the site, she got load of replies.
4 We won't be late. We've got plenty time.
5 There's hard any cheese left.
6 There are several of movies that he wants to watch.

3 Listen again. Are they speaking UK or US English?

1 ☐ 2 ☐ 3 ☐ 4 ☐ 5 ☐ 6 ☐

4 Underline one word which has a different spelling in US English. Write the US spelling above it.

1 I prefer going to the *theater* theatre to visiting museums.
2 We cycled approximately ninety-nine kilometres today.
3 E-catalogues aren't really necessary for online shopping.
4 She's studying Medicine and is specialising in dermatology, skin diseases and things like that.
5 We disliked all the design ideas and colours they suggested for our website.
6 Hello? Oh, Ian, hi! I really didn't recognise your voice! Are you sick?

5 Circle the correct option.

Carioca92:
Hi everyone! Can anyone tell me the difference between American and British English?

TeacherOnCall:
Hi Carioca! How are you doing? Despite all you might hear, there are actually only a ¹*few / little* big differences between them. ²*Plenty / Several* words are spelt differently, but they generally follow clear rules, such as the change in spelling from –*our* (UK) to –*or* (US). There are loads of different accents in US and UK English, for example Texan or Scottish, New York or London but generally, there are ³*hardly any / not much* words that are pronounced radically differently. Common examples are 'tomato' (UK: /təmɑːtəʊ/ US: /təmeɪtəʊ/) and 'schedule' (UK: /ʃedjuːl/ US: /skedʒuːl/), but using one pronunciation or the other won't confuse native speakers. There are, however, some differences that can cause ⁴*a bit of / many* confusion. For example, in the US, 'pants' means 'trousers' – in the UK, it means 'underwear for men'. This can create ⁵*lot of / some* problems. I can still remember being very surprised when an American friend told me he really liked my pants! Luckily, there isn't a large ⁶*number / quantity* of these words, but you should make a note of them whenever you come across them in class.

6 How do you pronounce the words in phonetics in ex 5? Listen and check.

Study tip

Check pronunciation of new words online or in a dictionary. Learning to read the phonetic alphabet makes this much easier. Use the chart on page 75 to help you.

Try too to notice and learn different spelling combinations for each sound. eg brainstorm different words with the same sound, then try to work out what's regular and what's an irregular spelling pattern for that sound. eg /əu/ has three regular spellings: *home* (O–consonant–E), *road*, (OA) *don't* (consonant–O–consonant) and an irregular one, OW, as in *slow* or *known*.

OW is normally pronounced /au/, as in *now*. Online rhyming dictionaries can help you with this too.

UNIT 4   101

4C Any volunteers?

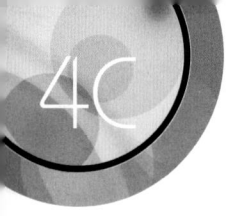

Vocabulary

Word Bank 18: Charity and the environment p.74
Nouns: challenge, cheetah, giraffe, security guard, volunteer, wastepaper basket,
Verbs: set up
Adjectives: ashamed, legendary, rewarding, rural
Expressions: in a race against time, to give birth

1 Complete the article with charity words.

A whale of a time

Ever since I was a small child I had been obsessed with whales, and I had always dreamed of seeing one. Then, one summer after I left school I saw an advert from a ¹non-g _ _ _ _ nm _ _ t _ _ organisation in the newspaper. It was a ²ch _ _ _ _ y that was inviting people to go on expeditions to observe bowhead whales to raise ³a _ a _ e _ _ _ s of the problems they have.

The bowhead whale is an ⁴_ _da_ g _ _ _ _ d species that lives off the coast of Canada and Greenland. Tragically, it is in danger of ⁵ex _ _ _ _ t _ _ _ as there are only about 10,000 left in the world. I was determined to help them so I agreed to work as a ⁶v _ _unt _ _ _ with the programme. However, first of all, I needed to do a bit of ⁷f _ _ dr _ _ _ _ ng because I needed to pay €2,000 to go on the trip. In the end, I ran the city marathon and got all my friends to ⁸sp _ _ s _ _ me.

2 True or false? Correct the false ones.

1 The purpose of fundraising is to teach the public about an NGO's work. ☐
2 Volunteers don't get paid for their work. ☐
3 Charities try to raise awareness of their work because it's important for them to work in secret. ☐
4 Both plants and animals can be endangered species. ☐
5 Environmental charities are trying to encourage the extinction of many wild animals. ☐
6 When an organisation sponsors someone, they pay them a salary. ☐

3 Circle the correct form, active or passive.

1 The fires *destroyed / was destroyed* hundreds of homes across the state.
2 Passports *checked / are checked* before passengers enter baggage reclaim.
3 The test results *have put / have been put* online.
4 A gang of burglars *arrested / was arrested* after an anonymous person called the police.
5 The printer *has run out / has been run out* of ink.
6 All the plants in the garden *killed / were killed* by the cold weather.

4 Complete the anecdote with the correct form of the verbs.

Just after I left college, I ¹_____ (employ) as a nurse by an NGO in Asia. At that time, all the children in the country ²_____ (give) vaccinations against a number of diseases. Well, one day, I ³_____ (ask) to go to the city hospital by my boss, because some important drugs for our clinic ⁴_____ (just / deliver). When I arrived, a man stood up and said 'hello', and I gave him my coat and hat. He looked slightly surprised but he hung them up for me. Although we ⁵_____ (not / introduce), he seemed to know my name and all about my work. But he asked so many questions that in the end, I just said "Look, I ⁶_____ (really / please) that you are so interested in our work but I came here for the drugs for our clinic. Could you go and get them for me, please?" At which point, he said "No, I don't think I will." I ⁷_____ (very / surprise) and I said "Why not?"

"You do know that I am this country's Minister of Health, don't you?" he said. I went bright red. Thankfully, just at that moment I saw that my drugs ⁸_____ (bring) into the room. I signed for them and left as quickly as I could.

5 (4.3) Mark the stressed syllable in the bold words in 1–3. Listen, check and repeat, making the links and copying the intonation.

1 We decided to **record** every part of the **project** on our website.
2 We're going to **project** photos of all these objects on the interactive whiteboard.
3 We wanted to break the world **record** for buskers playing together, but then the local government decided to **object** about the noise!

102

Reality TV ruined my life!

Vocabulary

Nouns: cartoon, deal, documentary, episode, failure, limousine, paradise, sitcom, soap opera
Verbs: launch, slip away, snap up
Adjectives: engaged, intense
Adverbs: incessantly
Expressions: a bit of a joke

1 Match the programme types and definitions.

> a cartoon __   A chat show __
> A documentary __   A science fiction series __
> A soap opera __

a a show where all the characters are drawings.
b a continuous programme, shown several times a week, with plenty of drama about ordinary life.
c a factual programme about e.g. wildlife or history.
d famous people are invited onto these to sit and talk to the presenter about their lives.
e usually set in the future, often with spaceships, etc.

2 Circle the correct option in the dialogue.

Julia Emin! If you ¹*didn't go / hadn't gone* on that TV show, our lives would be so much better. That reality show was a big mistake!

Emin What? But if I hadn't applied for the show, ²*I'd / 'll* still be working in the shoe shop. Now we're famous!

Julia You're famous. But not rich. If you'd sold your life story to the papers, ³*we'll / 'd* have a lot more money.

Emin But I'm writing a book about my time on the show. That'll make more money than some newspaper article.

Julia That book! It'll be all about you and that girl on the show. What was her name? Chardonnay or something?

Emin We've talked about all that. It's over now. If I ⁴*didn't pretend / hadn't pretended* to go out with her, people wouldn't want to read my book. TV's not real life. It was all for the cameras.

Julia You cynic! If you'd explained that to my mother, she ⁵*wouldn't be / wouldn't have been* so angry with you now! She was so embarrassed watching you and that girl on TV.

Emin Er, yeah, I'm sorry about that.

Julia And what about all these reporters! They wouldn't always ⁶*be hanging / have hung* around the house if you hadn't told the whole country our address on live TV! Look! There are three of them outside at the moment!

Emin Yeah, that was a mistake. Sorry.

Julia Sorry? You make my life hell and all you say is sorry!

3 (4.4) Listen and check. Pause after each of Julia's sentences and copy the intonation.

4 Match the sentences and cartoons. Which conditional form are they?

1 If you hadn't frightened him, he wouldn't be angry.
2 If I were you, I'd have the fish.
3 If you hadn't made so much noise, he wouldn't have seen us!

5 (4.5) Complete with prepositions and the verb phrases. Use contractions. Listen and check.

1 **A:** I can't believe you were ___ TV! You were great.
   B: Yeah, but I chose the wrong song and that's why I didn't win. If I had sung something different, I _____ the show next week. *(still / be)*

2 **A:** If I hadn't seen that documentary, I _____ about the destruction ___ the rainforest. *(know)*
   B: I know. It was shocking, wasn't it?

3 **A:** If there was something more interesting ___ the other channels, nobody _____ that stupid soap opera. *(watch)*
   B: That's not true. Lots ___ people really like it – like me, _____ instance!

4 **A:** If I hadn't left my mobile _____ home, I _____ Fatima and ask her ___ come over tonight. *(call)*
   B: I've got her number. I can call her if you like.

5 **A:** I was out last night so I missed the last episode _____ that sci-fi series.
   B: Oh no! I was watching it! If you had asked me, I _____ it _____ you. *(record)*

UNIT 4   103

4E My avatar and me

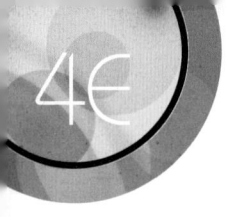

Vocabulary

Word Bank 19: Internet services p.74
Nouns: android, avatar, creator, panther, props, representation, slides, superhero, virtual, whiteboard
Verbs: manipulate, sketch, teleport   **Adjectives:** communicative, Hungarian, interactive, lifelike, willing
Expressions: an alter ego, from this point of view,

1 (4.6) Listen and match the company, type of website and the original language.

Company	Type of website	Original language
Allegro	e-tailer	Arabic
iWiW	video-sharing website	Hungarian
Marefa	social networking site	English
Erento	online encyclopedia	Polish
Goo	Internet telephony service provider	French
Ipernity	online auction site	Japanese
Ooma	search engine	German

2 Listen again and match the phrases to conversations 1 to 7. Check in (4.6) on p. 111. Shadow read the text, copying the links, stress and intonation.

> a bit similar to   far more fun than   just as successful as
> much easier if   not quite as famous as
> not nearly as well known as   slightly different to

3 Cross out the odd one out.
1 Buy things online using *an e-tailer / an online auction site / a search engine*.
2 Get facts and general knowledge using *an online encyclopedia / a social networking site / a search engine*.
3 Watch your family and friends online using *an e-tailer / a social networking site / a video-sharing website*.
4 Receive instant messages through *a social networking site / a video-sharing website / webmail*.
5 You don't need to log in to use *a search engine / a video-sharing website / webmail*.

4 Correct the typical mistakes with *one / ones* or articles.
1 **Customer:** How much is that top? No, not the lycra one, the cotton one.
   Assistant: Which? This short-sleeved or other one.
   Customer: I don't like white one. Can I try the other on, please?
2 **Customer:** I bought these trousers but they don't fit me. They're too small. Can I swap them for some different?
   Assistant: Which? Do you want same ones in a smaller size? Or a different style?

5 Add two more words to 1–7 and write them in the blog, *My Avatars and me*.
1 bit / more / crazy / others
2 nowhere / near / crazy
3 much / better / picture / others
4 don't / use / him / quite / often
5 just / strange / as / him
6 not / nearly / useful / Atahuapa
7 far / fun / design / than

My Avatars and me
Enrique Chavez

OK, I confess – I am a bit of a geek! I spend so much time online that I have four different avatars! The first one I call 'Quito'. He looks a ¹ _bit more crazy than the others_ because I use him for my English classes in Second Life. He's ² _____ my other avatars though...

The second one is called 'Atahualpa'. This image is a ³ _____ because I spent ages designing him. He looks like an Inca warrior from the 16th century because the Inca are from Peru, like me!

Then, er, well, then there's the rabbit, 'Conejito'. I ⁴ _____ Quito because I only play with him in one game with my little sister. Conejito may look odd but the avatars that the kids use ⁵ _____!

And finally we have the Joker. Actually, he's ⁶ _____ because he's difficult to operate. In fact, he was ⁷ _____ he is to use.

104

The Internet generation

Vocabulary

Word Bank 5: Adjective suffixes p.67
Nouns: arcade game, childhood, determination, jigsaw puzzle, substitute
Verbs: solve   **Adjectives:** sociable
Adverbs: partly   **Expressions:** in general, to change your mind

Test yourself on Unit 4

1. Do these exercises to check your progress.
2. Count your **correct** answers. Write the total number in the box.
   Total: ☐ /40 correct answers
3. Try to understand your mistakes. If necessary,
   - read the **Essential Grammar**, and / or
   - look at the Student Book lesson again, or
   - ask your teacher.
4. How do you feel after this unit? Tick (✓) a box.

---

1 Complete with these linkers. There are two extras.

| although | due | however | in spite of |
| instance | result | sum |

1. _____ the restaurant was really crowded, we still managed to get a table.
2. You can listen to our band's songs on loads of websites, for _____ YouTube or Spotify.
3. That's all I have to say. So, to _____ up, interactive whiteboards are completely changing the way we teach.
4. No one could access the Internet. As a _____, we had to cancel all lessons on the day.
5. The school was closed _____ to the bad weather.

2 Match the sentence halves.

1. An e-tailer is ☐
2. An online auction site is ☐
3. A search engine is ☐
4. Webmail is ☐
5. A social networking site is ☐

a. a site where you compete with other people to buy different things by raising the price you offer.
b. a way of sending and receiving messages wherever you are at any time and whatever computer you're on.
c. a company selling products only online like Play.com.
d. a place where you can post your own blog and photos as well as staying in contact with friends.
e. a site like Google that helps you to find information online.

I can use the future in the past. **Lesson 4A**

3 Add two missing words to each.

1. They going come at 6 pm but they've changed their plans.
2. I knew we wouldn't time to see everything while were in Budapest.
3. The exhibition to open June 1st but now it's opening a week later.
4. We couldn't go to the cinema because we meeting Boris the same time.
5. Front door was locked but I knew that Kurt have the key when he arrived.
6. I was about go in jeans and T-shirt when I realised the invitation said 'Wear formal clothes'.

I can use quantifiers with C and U nouns. **Lesson 4B**

4 Tick ✓ or correct the sentences.

1. There's hardly some time left!
2. We've had several visitors this afternoon.
3. We've got a few milk in the fridge.
4. There are large number of applicants for the new job.
5. We needs loads of plates because we've got over a hundred guests!
6. Clara told me she's got plenty money.

UNIT 4   105

4F

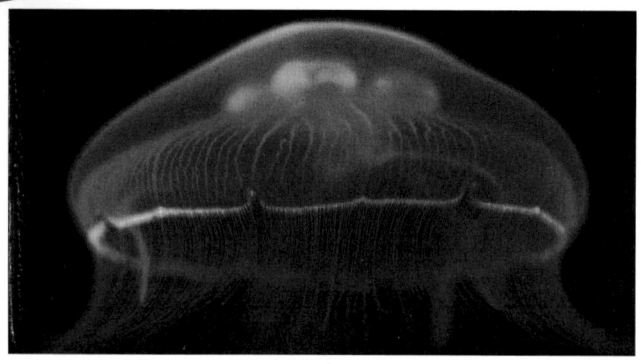

I can use the passive. (Lesson 4C)

5 Rewrite these sentences in the passive.

1 They'll open the doors at 3pm.

   The doors will be opened at 3pm.

2 A jellyfish stung me!

   _____

3 Nobody chose the course on Ancient Rome.

   _____

4 We are checking all the information on the computer.

   _____

5 The charity has asked various companies for help.

   _____

6 Chelsea aren't going to beat AC Milan.

   _____

7 Many people say that someone else wrote Shakespeare's plays.

   _____

I can use mixed conditionals. (Lesson 4D)

6 Complete the mixed conditionals with the verbs.

1 If I _____ to university when I left school, I'd have a much better job today. *(go)*

2 I would have something to read now if I _____ my book last night. *(not / finish)*

3 You _____ now at the weekend if you had done the work on Friday. *(not / work)*

4 If they had brought their warm coats, they _____ cold. *(feel)*

5 If my dad _____ German to me when I was a child, I'd be able to speak it perfectly today. *(speak)*

6 If we hadn't got this taxi, we _____ outside the station. *(still / wait)*

I can compare using adverbs. (Lesson 4E)

7 Circle the correct option.

1 This computer is *much / quite* quicker than the old one.

2 Hans is nowhere *near / nearly* as tall as Simon.

3 The sequel is *no / not* nearly as good as the original film.

4 We arrived a bit *early / earlier* than the others.

5 Mountain climbing is *far / lot* more exciting than skiing.

6 I think Tokyo is *just / much* as expensive as New York.

I can use a wide range of new vocabulary in English. (Lessons 4A–4F)

8 Can you remember...

1 **WB** Going to a gig? (p.73)

   16 words for concerts?

2 **WB** UK and US English (p.73)

   15 words that are different in UK and US English?

3 **WB** Charity and the environment (p.74)

   12 words or phrases for charities?

4 **WB** Internet services (p.74)

   9 different types of website?

5 **Phrasebook 4** (p.78)

   Can you use and pronounce well all 36 phrases?

6 All the new vocabulary from Lessons 4A–4E?

Audioscript

Student book

1.2 page 5

A Anja
I left school a year ago and I still haven't found a job. I've been looking for ages. I want to talk to my friends about it but I can't because I get so embarrassed. They've all got really good jobs and I'm the only one who hasn't. It's really depressing.

B Maria
I'm living with my parents. I moved back here after university. It was difficult at first because I had been living on my own – now, every time I do anything, my parents ask "Where are you going? What time are you coming home?" It's terrible. But what can I do? It's impossible to find a cheap apartment in Buenos Aries.

C Karen
I don't come from a rich family so I had to get student loans to pay for my college education. Now I'm thousands of pounds in debt and I worry about it all the time. Will I ever be able to pay it all back?

D Jelal
I took a degree in Media Studies but there weren't any jobs out there. So now, after the summer I'm going to work on my local newspaper – for free! It'll be a good way to make contacts and maybe get a proper job in the future. One that'll pay the bills!

E Bertil
When I took the job, I hadn't realised how boring it was. For example, today I was just typing information into a database, all day. So I've had enough. I'm leaving my job next week and I'm going travelling in Asia.

1.4 page 6

Zhu Zhu: I know that I'm his only child but I still don't understand why he calls me up all the time. He must ring me two or three times a day. It's ridiculous. And he tells me off if I don't call him– but I'm busy! He worries about me because I'm studying here in Switzerland, at a Hotel School. But, really, I'm fine. He wasn't like this when ¹I was growing up. Back home in China, he hardly ever spoke to me!

Lisa: It has to be my brother. I cannot understand how he manages to get the bathroom so dirty. When he has a shower, he gets water all over the floor … and he's always using my shampoo without asking me. We fall out over it all the time. Last week, he cut his nails and then left them in the sink. How disgusting is that! I can't put up with it any more. My parents don't do anything about it either! If I ever have children, ²I will not bring them up like that.

Claudia: My older brother broke up with his girlfriend recently, and since then he's always hanging around the house. He never goes out! I had thought ³that they always got on well together but now he spends all his time telling me how awful she was. It doesn't help that she's now going out with his best friend…

Ben: Well, ⁴I take after my dad. He's really relaxed, really good fun. I'm like that. But his father is the complete opposite. He's always telling me that I need to change my job or go back to university or do something else with my life. But I'm happy with my life now. The fact is that I can't live up to his expectations. It wouldn't be a problem but he lives right next door to us so I see him almost every day!

1.8 page 9

a: He əd booked all the accommədatən online.
b: We əd been walking in thə mountains all day.
c: That doesn't sound very comftəbəl.
d: While everyone wəs sleeping, I heard ə noise outside.
e: They wə thə people who əd booked thə house.
f: Becəse it wəs late and it wəs raining.

1.13 page 12

M = Mauro, N = Nancy

M: Another delay. It's always the same. If you get to the airport on time, the plane's always late.
N: It's only thirty minutes, Mauro. Let's get a coffee while we're waiting.
M: Yeah OK. What a pain, though.
N: Don't get stressed about it. If we didn't have planes, it would take a lot longer to get to Cape Town.
M: If we didn't have all these problems, I wouldn't be so fed up.
N: I should be fed up, not you. I'm only on this trip because Miranda's got the flu. Remember?
M: Yeah, I know.
N: So is something wrong today? You look a bit down. Is it the job? If there's anything wrong, I'll try and fix it for you.
M: No, no, it's not the job. I love it. We get to travel all around the world. We get to stay in expensive hotels. We get to meet famous people… Yeah. I'm happy.
N: But….?
M: But I heard from an old friend this week. Vanessa. We went to the international school together in London.
N: And?
M: Well, Vanessa has just finished drama school and now she's working as an actor! She's travelling the USA doing Shakespeare.
N: That's great news. Good for her!
M: But it's got me thinking, you see.

1.14 page 12

M: Well, Vanessa has just finished drama school and now she's working as an actor! She's travelling the USA doing Shakespeare.
N: That's great news. Good for her!
M: But it's got me thinking, you see.
N: Has it?
M: It's because I always wanted to be an actor. When I was a kid, that was my dream.
N: We all have those. I wanted to the first female president of the USA!
M: But you're not American, you're Canadian.
N: Children don't worry about things like that.
M: No. Anyway, now I'm thinking I made the wrong decision. Maybe I should be doing something else…
N: Really? Well, if you wanted to, you could give up your job and go to drama school. It's a big step though.
M: Yeah, and I'm earning good money now too. But I still think…
N: The grass is always greener on the other side.
M: What do you mean?
N: If you were an actor, you'd have a very stressful life. You'd probably want to come back to your old job.
M: But if I were in the theatre, I'd be doing something I love.
N: There are a lot of actors who never get near a theatre.
M: Vanessa did.
N: Then why don't you email her and ask her what it's like being a professional actor? Maybe it looks different from the inside.
M: Yeah, you're right. Wait… Is that our flight?

1.16 page 15

Nick: So Kate, you've finally decided to come to Greece. That's great news!
Kate: I'm really excited, Nick, but I'm a bit nervous too. That's why I phoned you up!
Nick: Nervous? Why? You'll love it! Greece is beautiful and the people are so friendly.
Kate: But I mean, I've never lived abroad before, and I'm flying out there next week!
Nick: Yes, but you're not alone. ¹I'm meeting you at the airport. When I arrived here, I didn't know anybody.
Kate: That's what I want to ask you. What was it like? What were your first impressions?
Nick: Well, I came to Athens, and that's very different to Paros, where you're going. Paros is a beautiful island. Athens is much more urban.
Kate: Is it?
Nick: Oh yeah. And when I arrived here in 2003, Athens was preparing for the Olympic Games. There was building work all over the city: people building new roads, new stadiums, everything. It was really polluted, and noisy too. But it's not like that now, because the Olympics are over.
Kate: So what are we going to do in Athens?
Nick: Well, ²my friend Yannis is going to drive us around the city and he's going to show us the sights. You know, the Acropolis, all the famous buildings.
Kate: Sounds lovely.
Nick: And in the evening we might go to Plaka. It's a bit touristy but it's still nice and you can eat some classic Greek food there.
Kate: Wonderful!
Nick: Now, how long are you staying in Athens?
Kate: Just a week. ³My ferry to Paros leaves on Monday morning.
Nick: Have you bought a ticket yet?
Kate: No, no, but I looked at the timetable online.
Nick: Well, don't get a ticket until you're in Athens. Sometimes the ferries don't run if it's stormy. You don't want to be hanging around the port all day if there's bad weather.
Kate: Is it OK to wait to buy the tickets?
Nick: Yes. ⁴There'll be lots of tickets on sale. You can turn up on the day to buy them.
Kate: OK. Great!
Nick: So do you have any other questions for me?
Kate: Oh, Nick, I've got hundreds.
Nick: Fire away then…

107

Audioscript

2.14 page 24

P = Presenter, YM = Young Man, YW = Young Woman,

P: OK, time for 'Money talks'. We're all tightening our belts at the moment with the economic crisis, so we went out to ask people if they know any other ways of making a little extra money.

YM 1: Well if you enjoy spending time with animals, you can earn good money just walking people's dogs. If you're strong enough, you can take several out at the same time – and charge the owners the same fee. I'm studying English here in London and it's a great way to make money when I'm not in class… and the payment is cash in hand too!

YM 2: Why not sell other people's stuff? Lots of people want to sell things on online sites like eBay. But, because they don't understand how to do it, they don't do it themselves. If you collect stuff from your friends and families, you can sell it and take a cut. Trust me, you'll soon be making serious money

YW: Lots of big companies need to know what's happening in their shops. So they send out people who pretend to be customers: the mystery shoppers. They then tell the company if the service is good or bad. If you're broke or if you just can't afford to eat in expensive restaurants or stay in big hotels, this may be perfect for you. You won't get a lot of money, but your expenses are all paid for.

YM 3: Well, one other thing you can do is to put advertising on your vehicle. It's an easy way to make a bit of money on the side. There are companies who will pay to put an advert on your car. So you can make money just driving around your home town, as long as you don't mind having some company's products all over your windows and doors!

2.18 page 27

(A = Businessman, B= Receptionist)

A: I'll be checking out at 5.30 tomorrow morning.
B: Certainly, sir.
A: I won't have time for breakfast.
B: There'll be some coffee ready in the lobby if you'd like some.
A: Great. And I'll get something to eat at the airport.
B: Shall I order you a taxi?
A: No, it's OK, thanks. My company will have booked a car for me.

2.22 page 28

Chris: As soon as I got in the car, I knew I would fail. It was the same examiner as before.
Jackie: You're joking!
Chris: No. And he must have remembered me, but he only said 'good morning' and we started the test. What happened first was that I hit the corner of the pavement just after we set off.
Jackie: Well, it could have happened to anyone.
Chris: Yeah. I might have failed the test then actually, but I thought, well, keep going…
Jackie: Right.
Chris: After that, there weren't any big problems… for a while. The examiner just gave instructions, 'turn left', 'turn right'. I was feeling pretty confident actually.
Jackie: Good for you.
Chris: Except that then, I drove the wrong way down a one way street.
Jackie: Oh no! How stupid! You can't have done that!
Chris: And the examiner stopped the car. I said 'You didn't tell me to turn.'
Jackie: And what did he say?
Chris: He said 'I thought it was obvious that you can't drive down this street.'
Jackie: So you failed.
Chris: It gets worse. We had stopped on a hill, and I had to reverse back up the hill. But I couldn't control the clutch or anything… and the examiner had to help me reverse the car. He took the steering wheel and directed us out.
Jackie: What a disaster! I would have been so embarrassed in that situation!
Chris: I *was* embarrassed. I should have waited before taking the second test, but that's life.

2.24 page 30

Elena: Chris, you're not in the office this afternoon, are you?
Chris: Er, no, Elena, I have a business meeting.
Elena: Really? Who with?
Chris: Er, Mary Peel.
Elena: Mary Peel. I've met her before, haven't I? At the sales conference in Chicago?
Chris: That's right. We all had dinner together.
Elena: I remember. Good looking girl, blonde. You went to university together, didn't you?
Chris: Er… yes. Wow, you've got a very good memory, Elena.
Elena: And you have a meeting with her. How interesting. What are you going to talk about? I mean she doesn't really work in our industry, does she? We make pet food, and she's…
Chris: A vet. I mean it's very similar. Vets are very important customers for pet food.
Elena: Uh-huh. I see. Are you meeting her here at the office?
Chris: Well, yes. It's what we normally do, isn't it?
Elena: Good! Then I can come along to your meeting too, can't I?
Chris: Er, no, well, I mean, that won't be necessary. I mean… we probably won't be talking about anything very important.
Elena: But I'd like to come along and see how you work. What time are you meeting her?
Chris: About 1 p.m.
Elena: That's about lunchtime, isn't it? I suppose it's a working lunch for you today.
Chris: Well, you know, I am very busy.
Elena: I'm sure you are. Right I'll see you later then, won't I?
Chris: Yes, Elena. Oh no!

3.2 page 33

L = Linus, S = Susannah

L: So here's my family. "The Sutters!" This picture is in Saint Gallen, that's my home town in Switzerland. This is my father…
S: Nice car.
L: Yeah, he's always driven a BMW. He loves his cars. He works for the government so he can afford it.
S: And your mum.
L: That's right. She works with the elderly. She's a… nurse. She works in the local hospital.
S: And this?
L: That? That's me!
S: You? But I wouldn't have… I wouldn't have recognised you!
L: This is me when I'm going to work.
S: But you look completely different!
L: By day, I'm an accountant, and by night, I'm a very different person.
S: Amazing.
L: It's because I work for a bank. So I have to wear a suit and tie. I leave my jewellery, my chains at home. I have to take the piercing out of… er this.
S: Your eyebrow.
L: Yeah! Eyebrow. Obviously, I need to wear long sleeves to cover my tattoos.
S: Right.
L: Very formal shoes.
S: And then at the weekend you wear completely different clothes!
L: That's right. I put on my boots, my leather jacket. I even use a different watch for work and for my free time. I've now shaved my head so I don't have to worry about my hair.
S: That's another reason why I didn't recognise you. You've got really curly hair in this photo!
L: I prefer it now.
S: Yeah? Anyway, Linus, the photos are great. You're a real Mario Testino.
L: Who's he?
S: He's a photographer from Peru. He's really famous. He does loads of celebrities.
L: Oh. I'll look him up on the Internet.
S: Yes, do that.

3.8 page 34

1
Fran: You're sniffing well.
Kevin: I think I'm coming down with something.
Fran: Would you like me to make an appointment with the doctor?
Kevin: Er… no I'm OK for now.
Fran: Right then. I'm off to work.

2
Kevin: Ooh… Oh.
Fran: How's the patient?
Kevin: I don't feel at all well.
Fran: Oh poor dear. Can I get you anything?
Kevin: Could you make me a cup of tea?
Fran: I suppose so.

3
Fran: Feeling better?
Kevin: I've got a sore throat.
Fran: Oh, you don't sound well today.
Kevin: Would you mind calling my boss?
Fran: No, I can do that. What's his number?
Kevin: It's on my mobile. Tell him I can't go to work.
Fran: You stay there. Don't move.

4
Fran: He'll call you tomorrow if he's better. OK, Bye.

108

Audioscript

Kevin: I've got a temperature of 39°.
Fran: Really? That's not good. You need some paracetamol to bring it down.
Kevin: Do you know if we have any in the house?
Fran: No, we don't. We've run out.
Kevin: Do you mind going to the chemist's to get some?
Fran: Yes, OK. But…
Kevin: What?
Fran: If you have a high temperature, it could be something serious. I was wondering whether you should go to the doctor.
Kevin: Yeah, you're right.

3.14 page 38

1 Dan and Lucy
D: Look at this picture! Where did you find it, Lucy?
L: It was in a book that I found upstairs. Someone must have put it there and forgotten it. It's great, isn't it? You don't wear checked trousers like that anymore, do you?
D: No! Mind you, Dad looks the same. I think he still has that shirt.
L: I think this is about 1974 or 1975, because I got that red dress for my birthday.
D: Wow, get you! Someone has a good memory.
L: Well I always liked clothes. In fact, I think clothes were much more fun back then. I wish people would wear clothes like that now.
D: We used to wear the most amazing things, didn't we? I wish mum and dad had taken more photos like this. I'd love to see them now.

2 Chris and Julie
C: Julie, can you believe we used to wear clothes like this … to school? Just look at us!
J: Well, you look OK in your yellow polo shirt and everything. But look at me in those purple trousers. What was I thinking of?
C: It's funny how things change, isn't it? Although, come to think of it, Luke's shirt does look pretty good. I mean checked shirts are always in fashion, aren't they? And you could probably wear the number 80 T-shirt today. What was his name?
J: Rick.
C: Uh-huh. I remember now. I'd love to send this picture to everyone. If only I had their emails.
J: Well, I don't like it at all, Chris. I wish you hadn't put it up on the web.

3 Tim and Chizuko
C: Tim! Look what I've found! I've never seen this picture before!
T: Ah, yes, Chizuko. That was my band back in the 1980s. Honestly, If only I hadn't worn that top. It seemed like a good idea at the time.
C: Are you the one with the saxophone?
T: Yeah, yeah, that was me. I wish I'd thrown that picture away.
C: Why? I love it! Look at the hair!

3.15 page 38

1: I wish people would wear clothes like that now.
2: I wish mum and dad had taken more photos like this.
3: If only I had their emails.
4: I wish you hadn't put it up on the web.
5: If only I hadn't worn that top.
6: I wish I'd thrown that picture away.

3.21 page 42

They say that many artists only become famous after they die. Well, that seems true for Congo, a chimpanzee who created over 400 paintings before he died at the age of 10 in 1964. Well, here we are today and Congo's work is more popular than ever. In one sale in London, three of his pictures beat the record price for animal art. The pictures were bought for £14,000, while a statue by Renoir wasn't even sold. Everyone's going crazy for Congo. So who exactly was Congo and why are people interested in his work?

3.22 page 42

So who exactly was Congo and why are people interested in his work? At the sale last week, I sought out Dusana Kurkova, an art expert from the Czech Republic.

P = Presenter, D = Dusana
P: Dusana, Is Congo the only animal artist that we know about?
D: No, there are several animals who have learnt to paint. But Congo is rather special. For example, an exhibition of ape art was held in London in 2005. Congo's pictures were hung next to others by a gorilla and a orang-utan too, but Congo's pictures were much better.
P: Why?
D: Look at the pictures. He hasn't just spread the paint everywhere. He's thinking about colours and shapes.
P: Uh huh. So how did Congo start painting?
D: Well, Congo was a zoo animal and he was looked after by a man called Desmond Morris. Now Morris encouraged Congo to paint and worked with Congo, taught him. For example, Morris chose different coloured paper for Congo to work with. Things like that. The colour of the paper make a big difference to the final picture.
P: So how did Morris get Congo to paint? I imagine he fed Congo special foods as a reward, or something like that.
D: No, that's not true. I think Congo painted because he enjoyed it. He didn't just paint either. He also drew with a pencil. He was a very creative monkey.
P: What did real artists think about his work?
D: Lots of them loved it. They say that Picasso actually owned one of Congo's pictures himself.
P: I have to say, I think I probably prefer Congo's paintings to Picasso's. Thanks Dusana.

So there we go, the work of Congo. Log on again next week when we look at another unusual story that's been in the news.

4.3 page 47

Phil
You're not going to believe this but… er, the first gig I ever saw was Nirvana. I can't remember the exact date because it was so long ago. I don't think that I knew who Nirvana were. It was my brother, you see. He was going to see a gig with his then girlfriend. But they had had this enormous row and in the end, she wasn't going to go to the concert. Well, my brother had two tickets and he still wanted to go. So he asked me. I was only eighteen and he was three years older. So we went along to the venue and we saw this amazing gig. Incredible. And the atmosphere was awesome. I mean I've been to a lot of gigs and a lot of gigs and festivals since then, but that first one was the best. I never saw him again though. I remember in 1994, Nirvana were to play in the Lollapalooza festival. I wanted to see him but they cancelled the gig. And Kurt Cobain died the next day, I think. 27. A tragic loss.

Estefania
My cousin's band. I saw them last week. It was in our school sports hall, here in São Paolo. I went with my friend Luiza. We thought there would be lots of people there but it was empty. It was a complete disaster. I know what went wrong too. They wanted to put up posters to tell everyone they were having a concert. But they asked the drummer to do it and he forgot. I knew he wouldn't do it. He's a bit lazy really. Anyway, there were about twenty of us there and we watched them play, maybe, seven songs, and that was it. They didn't do any encores or anything. It was not exactly rock and roll. They've got another gig next week as the support act for another band, but I think I'll stay at home for that one.

Judy
I went with my friends to see Coldplay last year! They were great! My friends got the tickets for my birthday. I knew the present was going to be concert tickets but I didn't know which band it would be. And Coldplay! It was so cool. Because we live in a small town… we don't live in a big city or anything like that… So I'd never been to a concert before and the whole thing was just so good. They sound even better live than on CD and Chris Martin's singing was fantastic. The set list was perfect: all my favourites like *Yellow* and *Green Eyes*. There was one scary moment, though, when we were travelling to the gig. When we were leaving the car park in my home town, another car almost crashed into our coach! I thought we were going to crash! Luckily nothing happened, and we got there OK in the end.

4.6 page 48

H = Hannah, J = Jong Kyu
H: What's that? Are you taking music lessons?
J: Yes! I've been going to guitar classes.
H: When did you start that?
J: It was after I got my Wii system. I had hardly any games when I started but I did have Guitar Hero 5. I loved it. I was playing it all the time.
H: All the time?
J: Yeah. I got a bit obsessed, actually. I was playing it with other people online in a band. One person's the singer, another's the drummer…
H: You play with other people online? Surely there are plenty of people who'd play Guitar Hero with you here? Real people… in the same room as you?
J: Er… yes. But they don't always like playing it all night long.
H: All night?
J: The other people in my band are in Australia so I can play with them when everyone here is asleep. We're really good now and we've completed loads of songs together. So then, I thought, now I want to learn the guitar. I need to play. I need an audience.
H: You need a doctor if you've been playing computer games all night long.
J: You used to spend a large amount of time online at night yourself.
H: I was doing my university project! That's a bit different, isn't it?
J: Well anyway, *Guitar Hero 5* has changed my life!

109

Audioscript

4.7 page 48

Doctor: So what can I do for you today?
Theo: It's my arm, doctor.
Doctor: Oh yes? It's been giving you a bit of pain, has it? Where exactly does it hurt you?
Theo: It's my shoulder.
Doctor: What do you think has caused it?
Theo: Well, I think…
Doctor: Yes?
Theo: I think it might be my computer tennis game.
Doctor: You mean like on the game system?
Theo: Yes, that's right.
Doctor: Do you spend a lot of time playing this game then?
Theo: I have been playing it a lot recently.
Doctor: You've been playing it so much that you've hurt your arm?
Theo: Well I have a very stressful job, you see…
Doctor: Uh huh.
Theo: … and I need **a little** time to relax when I get home. So I always play a game or two on the computer for **a few** hours or so…
Doctor: Do you only have one game?
Theo: Well, I've played **several of** the other games but they're not as good as the tennis one.
Doctor: Well, I suggest you stop playing it for a while and try one of the others.
Theo: Aren't you going to give me some medicine?

4.13 page 51

Linda: No. Now, tell us about your volunteering. You were a teacher?
James: That's right. I'm a teacher here in the UK, so I was just doing the same job in another country. My classes were twelve years and younger.
Linda: What were the schools like?
James: I was in a rural area and there weren't a lot of resources. I took a lot of books with me as a **present** to give to the school. Er… It was a challenge as a teacher because I had to do things very differently, but you get used to that.
Linda: Do you have any funny stories to tell us?
James: Yes. One morning, I saw this strange **object** in the wastepaper basket. I was about to pick it up when I saw it was a snake!
Linda: Was it dangerous?
James: Maybe. There are a dozen deadly snakes in Botswana. Anyway, all the children ran out of the room and eventually it was removed by the father of one of the children!
Linda: Incredible. Was there anything you found difficult when you there?
James: The heat. I lived in a simple house with no air conditioning, and sometimes no water. Some days it was incredibly hot. The record when I was there was 40o centigrade.
Linda: Wow. And now you **present** talks on volunteering in Africa.
James: Yes. It's very important to raise awareness of what is happening in Africa and what people need there. I also do a lot of fundraising. We ask people to sponsor a particular child in a school for example, to pay for equipment and things like that.
Linda: How would you advise other people to work as volunteers in somewhere like Botswana?
James: I would say that it's a great experience. One thing I would say is that it is a very different culture to the UK and you need to be prepared for that. Many people **object** to things like piercings, for example. But if you do plenty of research before you go, you won't have any problems. And most of all, if you do volunteer to do something like this, you'll find that it's a very, very rewarding experience.
Linda: Sounds great! Thank you James.

4.14 page 52

1 Heinz, Frankfurt
The Simpsons is my favourite show. Every single week it is just so, so funny. I first saw it at school and I got hooked. I used to draw all the characters and write my own little stories about them. In fact, that's how I started out in my career. Because I now work on a cartoon series here in Germany. And I'm sure that if I hadn't been a *Simpsons* fan, I wouldn't be a cartoonist today.

2 Natalie, Rouen
It's a bit sad I know, but I am ob**sessed** with a show that we call *Summer Bay* and you call in English… It's called *Home and Away*. It's all about people **my age**, young people who live by the sea and their **everyday** lives in Australia. Whenever it's on, I **have to be** at home and watching it. I like it because the characters live **such fantastic lives** in such a beautiful place. I can watch the show and I can **dream** a little bit. If I had been born in Australia, I **would love to live** somewhere like that.

3 Bethany, Dublin
Well, it's a British TV show but we can watch here too in the Republic. *Shipwrecked*. Ah, it's great. There are two teams and they live on two separate desert islands. One team is called the Tigers and the other team is called the Sharks. Every week a new person joins the show. Er… and the new person chooses a team. What's astonishing is that a friend of mine is on the show now, as we speak! Imagine that. If I had applied for the show, I could be on the TV now too, living in paradise.

4 Alberto, Lima
I'm addicted to *Mad Men*. It's set in an advertising company in New York in the 1960s. I just love it because life in the 60s seems so different to life today. The things that people say and do at work are incredible. When it first came out, I missed it because I was working in the evenings. Luckily, one of my colleagues, Alison, recorded it for me every week. We were always talking about the show together and then, we became friends. We started going out together and now we're engaged! So you see, if I had never watched *Mad Men*, I wouldn't be getting married now.

4.20 page 58

1
A: How was the party?
B: It was a disaster! There was hardly anyone there. We were in this huge club with just half a dozen of us talking.
A: Oh, that doesn't sound very good.
B: But I ran into Suzie in the lift when I was going home and we went out to another disco… which was much more fun.
A: Oh yeah?

2
Woman: Oh that's nice. Is that a new mobile? A Nokia?
Man: Yeah. I always get them.
Woman: It looks very unusual doesn't it?
Man: That's OK for me. The only thing is I can't see how to use several of the special features.
Woman: Give it to me. I know all about this sort of thing.

3
Mother: You got those biscuits out of the oven just in time.
Girl: Yeah, they're ready! Do you want to try one?
Mother: Mmm, they smell delicious. They don't have loads of sugar in, do they?
Girl: No, no, they're very healthy. They're lemon. Go on try one.
Mother: OK, erm, oh, er… It's a bit salty.
Girl: Do you like them?
Mother: Give one to your father.

4
Girl: Who was that girl at the party, Ricky? Does she go to our school?
Ricky: Er… no. I met her on Facebook. She's the friend of a friend.
Girl: Are you going out with her?
Ricky: No. We broke up just after the party, actually.
Girl: Well, don't worry. There's plenty of fish in the sea. Give it a little time and you'll meet someone else.
Ricky: Yeah, yeah, that's what everyone says.
Girl: No, it's true. I met my boyfriend when I was waiting in a queue at the cinema…

Activity book

3.3 page 94

Teacher: Olga? Do you know if anyone else is coming to class today?
Olga: Er, I don't know Mr Barnes. Would you like me to see if anyone else is waiting in the corridor?
Teacher: No, no, that's all right. You stay where you are. I was wondering if I was in the right classroom.
Olga: I think so. It's just that… lots of people are off sick.
Teacher: Hmm… interesting coincidence. Today, we have a very difficult test and everyone in the class is away sick. Were you at the school disco yesterday?
Olga: Er … yes.
Teacher: Would you mind telling me how many other people were there?
Olga: I think everyone in our class was there, Mr Barnes.
Teacher: Were they? How interesting. Could you see if they were sick? Did they look a little unwell?
Olga: Oh no, everyone looked fine. they were having a great time.
Teacher: I see. Well at least you're here.

110

Audioscript

Olga:	Actually, I don't feel very well myself. Do you mind if I go and see the school nurse?
Teacher:	In my day, we didn't take days off just because we felt a bit ill.
Olga:	But that was a long time ago, wasn't it, Mr Barnes?
Teacher:	What?

3.7 page 97

1	Woman	Is that box of plastic dinosaurs for you?
	Man	No! It's for the kids this afternoon. They need something to play with.
	Woman	That's a good idea, they'll enjoy that!
2	Man	Oh no. It's raining and we have to go through fields and woods.
	Woman	Oh, stop complaining. Put on your rubber boots and let's go.
3	Woman	It's time to go to the factory.
	Man	Sorry?
	Woman	It's time to go to the factory!
	Man	All right, all right. There's no need to shout.
	Woman	Your hearing is getting worse. It must be really noisy making those steel cables.
	Man	Yeah. It is.
4	Woman	Oh, I like your lycra shorts.
	Man	Hmm… I only wear them on the bike. Everyone in the club wears them.
	Woman	Really?
5	Woman 1	Look at this. We're all wearing these pink silk dresses. They're beautiful.
	Woman 2	Wait until you see what the bride is wearing.
6	Man	Ah, if you're taking the rubbish out, can you take this bag of aluminium cans too?
	Woman	Oh, they're a bit heavy.
	Man	Yeah, sorry. I always leave it, and that's why there's so much of it.
	Woman	Well, why don't you take it out more often, then?

4.1 page 100

1
A: When I go to gigs, I don't usually bother to watch the support act, as they're usually terrible. But when I heard it was to be Snow Patrol, I went along 'cos I thought they'd be good.
B: Were they?
A: Yeah, brilliant! I reckon they should have been headlining. I mean, they were awesome.

2
A: On the ticket, it looked like we were sitting in a part of the stadium with a roof.
B: That's not true. None of the seats in that venue are under a roof.
A: Well I know that now, and it rained all through the concert.
B: Oh no!

3
A: I didn't know what the gig was going to be like because I'd never really listened to Robbie Williams on CD.
B: How was it in the end?
A: The best gig of my life. He's an incredible live performer: his songs are OK and everyone knows every word, but he really knows how to work a crowd. And his eyes are just so attractive. Amazing.

4
A: I heard that lots of people were complaining about the sound.
B: Yeah, the bass and drums were both a bit too loud. But otherwise, I thought it was OK. The problem for me was that we couldn't see the stage. There were loads of really tall guys in front of me.
A: That's really annoying!
B: Yeah! I hate it. But I knew it would be a problem because thousands of people were going the gig. I just wish I was a bit taller!

5
A: How was the gig? Was it good?
B: They sounded OK and the band was good … but the set list was terrible. If I'd known that they were only playing songs from their new album, I wouldn't have gone.
A: They didn't play any of their hits?
B: The only song I knew was the encore. That was magic!

4.6 page 104

1: Although_it's not QUITE_as Famous_as EBay, ALLEgro_is POland's_OWN_Online_AUction WEBsite. It was FOUNded_in NINEteen, NINEty-NINE and has become_inCREdibly POpular there. And_it alREAdy Operates_in at least TEN_other countries. Who knows how_it might grow_in the future?

2: EVERYbody knows Facebook but there_are many_other social networking sites_out there. One_example_is iWiW from HUNGary, which has_over 4 MILlion_users. This means that_in_its_own country, iWiW_is JUST_as successful_as Facebook

3: Although_at the moment, it's nowhere near_as well known_as WikiPEDia, MaREFa_is_another_example_of_an online_ encyclopedia that _is written by_its_users. It_is written_in_ARabic and_is_available free online.

4: Erento_is_an_e-tailer, based_in BerLIN, Germany. However, it's slightly DIFFerent to companies like_AMazon because_it RENTS products rather than selling them. The range_of products_available_is_inCREDible – anything from computers to cars. If you can rent_it, it's probably on_Erento.

5: Looking for_information_online_is much_ easier_if you can just write your request_in your own_ALPHabet_or LANGuage. There_are plenty_of sites_available around the world for people who DON'T speak_English_as their first language. For_example. if you're looking for information_online_in Japanese, the search_engine for YOU may be GOO.

6: Putting your photos_and videos_online_is far more fun than keeping them to yourself. For_amateur photographers_and diRECtors like myself, I can recommend Ipernity. It's_a video-sharing website designed by two French programmers, and_I_absolutely LOVE_it!

7: I hardly_ever use my land line these days. I just make calls_over the Net, using_a site called_OOma. It's_a bit similar to Skype. It's great for making calls_inside the US, and_in fact_it's from the States. AWEsome!

111

1 Essential Grammar

Tense review → 1A

1 Write the missing tense names 1–4.

Present simple	I **live** / **don't live** in Scotland
1 _____	We **enjoyed** / **didn't enjoy** the film.
Future simple	I'll **see** / **won't see** you tomorrow night.
2 _____	They**'ve** / **haven't** started eating.
Past perfect	He**'d** / **hadn't** finished speaking.
Present continuous	She**'s** / **isn't leaving** home.
Present perfect continuous	He**'s** / **hasn't been waiting** a long time.
Past continuous	We **were** / **weren't speaking** English.
3 _____	It**'d** / **hadn't been snowing**.
4 _____	They**'ll** / **won't be standing** outside.
Going to	I**'m (not) going to have** lunch at home.

2 True or false?

1 Every simple tense has both a *continuous* and a *perfect* form.
2 Continuous forms all include *–ing*, and emphasise an action in progress.
3 Non-action verbs (e.g. *know*, *think*, *believe*, *like*) aren't normally used in continuous forms.
4 To make a future form, you must use *will*.

3 Circle the correct option.

1 *Did you speak / Have you spoken* to Ibrahim yesterday?
2 In the Middle Ages, people *believed / were believing* the earth was flat.
3 *I give / I'll give* you my mobile number, so you can call me later on.

Phrasal verbs → 1B

A phrasal verb = verb + particle (*at*, *away*, *for*, etc.).
There are four types:

Separable	I'm **filling in** the form. / I'm **filling** it **in**.
Inseparable	We're **looking after** my neighbour's cat.
Intransitive (no object)	The car**'s broken down**.
Three part	I **look forward to** your reply.

4 Complete the rules with these words.

> after   inseparable   particle   pronoun

Rules

'Separable' means the object can go after the phrasal verb, or between the verb and particle. If the object of the phrasal verb is a ¹_____ it must go between the verb and the ²_____.

Three part phrasal verbs are ³_____. The object must go ⁴_____ the phrasal verb.

Narrative tenses → 1C

a	Past continuous	While I **was looking** for my keys, I…
b	Past simple	… **heard** a strange noise inside the room. I suddenly **felt** scared…
c	Past perfect continuous	… because **we had been having** a lot of burglaries in our area.
d	Past perfect	Even though I knew everybody **had** already **gone** home, I called out 'Hello'…

5 Match rules 1–4 to the four narrative tenses, a–d.

☐ 1 The most common past tense. Use it to tell the events of a story in order: 1, 2, 3…
☐ 2 For an action that begins and possibly continues after another past action.
☐ 3 To refer to events that happened before another past time.
☐ 4 For actions that continue for a long time before another past time.

6 Improve the verbs in bold with narrative tenses.

1 Sam didn't get your email until 5 pm because he **worked** *(was working)* from home and his computer **didn't work** properly.
2 I couldn't do any work because my neighbours **argued** all day. I couldn't hear what they **said** but they **shouted** at each other for hours.
3 It still **snowed** when the girls woke up. They jumped out of bed and looked out the window. Their father **already got up** and he **made** a snowman in the front garden.

1

be used to, get used to → 1D

be used to	We **are used to** eating lots of spicy food. He wasn't **used to speaking** English on the phone.
get used to	I **haven't got used to living** away from home. Jana **can't get used to** starting work at 5 am.

7 Match the sentence halves to make rules 1–3.

1 *Be used to* and *get used to* are both
2 *Be used to* means something is
3 *Get used to* means something is

a followed either by the gerund (*-ing*) or a noun. ☐
b becoming familiar, (not normal yet). ☐
c already familiar, but it was not in the past. ☐

8 Complete with *be* or *get* in the right tense.

1 They couldn't get to sleep because they _____ used to sleeping in a tent.
2 Chikako _____ slowly _____ used to her new school. Everything's still very new, though.
3 I don't think I _____ ever _____ used to wearing this stupid uniform!
4 Gabriel _____ used to eating late so he won't mind having dinner at 11.

Zero, first and second conditionals → 1E

9 Complete the grammar chart.

Zero	If it rains	you ¹_____ wet.
First	If you clean the living room	I ²_____ clean the bathroom.
Second	If I ³_____ you	I wouldn't leave now.

10 Circle the correct rules.

1 The zero conditional describes situations that are always *changing / true*.
2 The first conditional describes *realistic / impossible* situations.
3 The second conditional describes *very probable / hypothetical* situations.

The future → 1F, 2E

English has many future tense forms. More than one future is often possible in the same situation. A common mistake is to over-use *will*.

Will = simple predictions and spontaneous decisions	I think it**'ll be** a nice day tomorrow. Oh, the phone's ringing. I**'ll answer** it!
Present simple = timetabled events or schedules	Check in **starts** at 9.20 pm.
going to = predictions, especially when there's present evidence	Look at those clouds. It**'s going to rain**.
going to = future plans	We**'re going to visit** Vietnam in April.
Present continuous = future arrangements, especially ones made with other people.	Mike**'s coming here** for a meeting at lunchtime tomorrow.

11 Correct these typical mistakes with *will*.

1 I'll see the dentist at 6.35 on Thursday.
2 It's 4–0 with five minutes left to play. We'll win the match!
3 I'm sending out invitations because we'll have a surprise party for my grandma.
4 The library will open at 9 and will close at 4 all next week.

---

1 1 Past simple 2 Present perfect 3 Past perfect continuous 4 Future continuous
2 1 T 2 T 3 T 4 F
3 1 Did you speak 2 believed 3 I'll give
4 1 pronoun 2 particle 3 inseparable 4 after
5 1 b 2 a 3 d 4 c
6 1 his computer hadn't been working properly.
2 neighbours were arguing, they were saying, they were shouting
3 It was still snowing, father had already got up, he had made
7 1 a 2 c 3 b
8 1 aren't 2 is, getting 3 'll, get 4 is
9 1 get 2 will 3 were
10 1 true 2 realistic 3 hypothetical
11 1 I'm seeing 2 We're going to win 3 we're going to have 4 opens, closes

113

2 Essential Grammar

Relative clauses → 2A

Defining relative clauses	I really enjoyed the film **(that) we watched last night**.
Non-defining relative clauses	The only person online was Lee, **who was answering emails**.

1 Complete the rules with these words.

> comma   exactly   noun   possession   reasons   that

1. Relative clauses (RCs) give more information about a _____ or a sentence.
2. RCs can begin with *who*, *which*, *that*, *where*, *when*, and *whose* (for _____).
3. A defining RC tells us _____ what a noun is.
4. A non-defining RC gives us extra information about a noun. It's separated from the rest of the sentence with a _____.
5. In defining RCs, *why* can be used to explain _____.
6. In defining RCs, *who*, *which*, _____ etc., may be left out if they're the **object** of the clause, except for *where* and *whose*.

2 Add one word in the correct place.

1. Marie, *whose* mother is French, agreed to do the translation for us.
2. I don't know the reason everyone was late.
3. I saw that Ravi's house, we had the barbecue last year, is for sale.
4. A smoothie is a drink is made from fruit juice and yoghurt.
5. I remember the day my nephew was born very clearly.
6. The boy sailed solo round the wrold was only 15.

Question tags → 2B

> Form Q tags with the main verb + a pronoun.
> Q tags are usually: positive sentence, positive tag; negative sentence, negative tag.

3 Write the tags.

1. It's a secret. You won't tell anyone, _____?
2. I'm going to win the competition, _____?
3. You'd met Viktor before, _____?

Reported speech and reported questions → 2C

4 Complete the table.

Direct speech	Reported speech
Present simple *I don't smoke*	Past simple *I didn't smoke*
Present continuous *I'm going out*	1 _____
Past simple *I had breakfast*	2 _____
Past continuous *He was working*	3 _____
Present perfect *We've finished*	4 _____
Past perfect *I'd done it*	Past Perfect *I'd done it* (no change)
is / are going to	*was / were going to*
will / can / must	5 _____

NB In reported speech, all tenses become past perfect except the present, future and modals.

5 Rewrite in reported speech.

1. Nuria: "I have a problem."
   Nuria said she had a problem.
2. Toshi: "I hadn't heard the news."
   _____
3. Walter: "I can't speak French."
   _____
4. Isa: "Are you looking for someone?"
   _____
5. Zak: "Where is our classroom?"
   _____
6. Dominic: "Susan has already finished her project."
   _____

When reporting speech, you often need to change **time** and **place** references.

now / today / tonight / this week	then / that day / that night / that week
yesterday / last week / last month	the day before / the week before / the month before
tomorrow / next week / next month	the next (or following) day / the week after / the month after
here / this place / these places	there / that place / those places

114

6 Complete by changing the words in brackets into reported speech.

1 Jay said that he had only been _____ for about five minutes _____. (here / yesterday)
2 He told me _____ was the first time he'd arrived home late _____. (this / this week)
3 And he said that he wasn't going back to _____ _____. (this hotel / next year).

Verb patterns → 2D

7 Are these verbs + gerund (G), + infinitive (I), or + both gerund or infinitive (B)?

agree (I)   avoid (G)   can't stand   choose   decide   deny
dislike   enjoy   expect   feel like   involve   love
manage   miss   prefer   pretend   stop   tend   try

Future: Simple, Continuous or Perfect for predictions → 2E

Future simple	It'll / won't be cold tomorrow.
Future continuous	He'll / won't be leaving tomorrow.
Future perfect	I'll / won't have finished by midnight.
Future perfect continuous	They'll / won't have been waiting too long by the time we arrive.

8 Match functions 1–5 with sentences a–e.

1 A prediction or a single future event. ☐
2 An action in progress at a future point. ☐
3 Speculating about an action in progress at the moment of speaking. ☐
4 An action that happens for a long time before a future time. **b**
5 An action or event that happens before a future time. ☐

a They said their plane lands at 11 a.m. local time so they'll just be arriving now.
b By the time we get to Milan, we'll have been cycling for over five hours!
c This time next week, we'll be lying on a beach in Bali.
d We can't use our new kitchen before June because they won't have finished building it.
e It'll be a nice day tomorrow.

You can also use the future continuous to describe future arrangements, in the same way as the present continuous: *Shakira will be signing copies of her latest album at this store all day tomorrow.*

Past modals → 2F

Most modal verbs have the same meaning in the present and past.

I can't help → I **couldn't have** helped you.
They might miss → They **might have missed** the bus.

To hypothesise about the past, use
– *must have done* when you're sure it happened.
– *can't have done* when you're sure it <u>didn't</u> happen.

9 Complete with the verbs in the past.

1 They _____ (have to / get up) at 6 am this morning so they _____ (might / leave) already.
2 Why did you walk to the supermarket? You _____ (should / call) me. I _____ (would / drive) you there.
3 The visitors _____ (can't / come) through the front door. It's not possible. They _____ (must / arrive) round the back.

---

9 1 had to get up, might have left   2 Should have called, would have driven   3 can't have come, must have arrived
8 1 e   2 c   3 a   4 b   5 d
7 + gerund: avoid, can't stand, deny, dislike, enjoy, feel like, involve, miss
Both: love, prefer, stop, try
+ infinitive: agree, choose, decide, manage, pretend, tend
6 1 there, the day before   2 that, that week   3 that hotel, the year after
5 1 said he hadn't heard the news.   2 said he couldn't speak French.   3 asked whether I was looking for someone.   4 asked where our classroom was.   5 said Susan had already finished her project.
4 1 Past continuous   2 Past perfect   3 Past perfect continuous   4 Past perfect   5 would / could / must
3 1 will you   2 aren't I   3 hadn't you
2 1 when / that my   2 why everyone   3 where we had   4 which / that is made   5 who sailed solo
1 1 noun   2 possession   3 exactly   4 comma   5 reasons   6 that

115

3 Essential Grammar

Articles → 3A

1 Match examples a–f with rules 1–6.

a I've got <u>a new email</u>. ☐
b Kim's <u>at university</u> in Geneva. ☐
c There's a problem with <u>the car</u>. ☐
d There's something wrong with <u>my contact lenses</u>. ☐
e Dubai is in <u>the United Arab Emirates</u>. ☐
f I'm a big fan <u>of Asian cinema</u>. ☐

Definite *(the)*, indefinite *(a / an)* and zero articles	
1	Use *the* when both speaker and listener know which one(s).
2	Use *a / an* when which one (NOT ones) isn't clear.
3	Don't use *the* for possessions and parts of the body. Use *my*, *your*, *his*, etc.
Use zero article:	
4	to talk **in general** about both U nouns and plural C nouns
5	for most names, except **certain countries, places & locations**, which you need to learn.
6	for places where people form part of a community, eg *church*, *hospital*, *prison*, and *school*. BUT Use *the* for these places when you work there or are referring to the building.
Note these further phrases with no article: *go home*, *go to work go to bed*.	

Indirect questions → 3B

2 Circle the correct rule.

1 Use an indirect question to be more *informal / formal* and polite.
2 Word order in indirect questions is *the same as / different to* direct questions.
3 Questions with *I was wondering whether* end with *a full stop (.) / a question mark (?)*.

> Would you like someone to help you?
> Could you give me some advice?
> Would you mind waiting for a couple of minutes?
> Do you know if there are any problems?
> Do you mind staying at a cheaper hotel?
> I was wondering whether we should send everyone an email.

3 Rewrite as an indirect question.

1 I can help you tidy up.
   Would you like me <u>to help you to tidy up</u> ?
2 We need to wrap Nina's birthday presents.
   Could you _____ ?
3 Does Ros live in the same house as Sam?
   Do you know if _____
4 It's cheaper to fly with a budget airline.
   Do you mind _____

Present perfect continuous → 3C

| He | has / hasn't | been working | in the garden. |

Use the present perfect continuous for...	
actions which began in the past and continue into the present.	It's **been raining** for hours!
actions which took place over a long time, and which have a present result.	My clothes are covered in paint because **we've been decorating**.
When you talk about the amount of things that you have done, use the Present Perfect Simple.	**I've sent** over a hundred emails today.

4 Describe situations A–C. Use the Present Perfect Continuous.

116

3

Wishes and regrets → 3D

5 Complete the examples with verbs.

Present wishes and regrets

I wish	I had	my own car.
	you ¹_____ arrive	to class on time!
If only	I ²_____	rich!
	he **would call**	me!

Past wishes and regrets

I wish	I ³_____ left	my laptop on the train.
If only	we ⁴_____ had	more time!

6 Correct these typical mistakes.

1 I wish you will do the washing up occasionally!
2 I wish I worked harder when I was at school.
3 I'm wishing I had never taken this job!
4 If only we would get some news from Laura from time to time.
5 If only he helps me more often.
6 If only he told me this yesterday!

The third conditional → 3E

Use the third conditional to describe hypothetical situations in the past. Form it with modals *would*, *could* or *might*.

Third conditional	If you **had been** there, you **would have loved** it. If I'**d had** more money, I **could have bought** that book. If you **had said** 'hello' to her, she **might have said** 'hello' back.

7 Complete with the verbs. Use contractions.

1 We _____ the league if the other team hadn't scored in the last minute! *(win)*
2 If I _____ in Ancient Rome, I'd have loved to have been an Emperor. *(lived)*
3 We _____ to Wembley too, if we'd had more time in London. *(could / go)*
4 Mum wouldn't have known about that broken vase if you _____ her about it! *(not / tell)*
5 If you'd come on the trip with us, you _____ it. *(might / enjoy)*

Further irregular verbs → 3F

8 Write the past simple and participles of these verbs. Check your answers on page 76.

beat   bite   blow   burn   buy   choose   creep   draw   feed   freeze   hang   hide
hold   quit   ride   seek   shake   shoot   shut   spread   stand   sting   wake   wear

---

1 a 2 b 6 c 1 d 3 e 5 f 4
2 1 formal and polite. 2 different to 3 a full stop (.)
3 2 Could you wrap Nina's birthday presents?
3 Do you know if Ros lives in the same house as Sam? 4 Do you mind flying with a budget airline?
4 Possible answers
1 She's been cleaning the house. 2 They've been snowboarding. 3 He's been watching a football match.
5 1 would 2 were 3 hadn't 4 had
6 1 you would do 2 I had worked 3 I had never taken 4 we got some 5 he helped me 6 he had told me
7 1 'd have won 2 'd lived 3 could have gone 4 hadn't told 5 might have enjoyed

117

4 Essential Grammar

The future in the past → 4A

Follow the same rules as reported speech (EG2, ex 4, p. 114). Move the future verb one tense back.

Original intention	The future in the past
Present continuous: **I'm giving up**	Past continuous: **I was giving up**
Be going to: **We aren't going to work**	**We weren't going to work**
Will: **He'll never do it**	**He would never do it**
be to: **They're about to leave**	**They were about to leave**

1 Complete captions 1–4 with the verb. Use each form of the future in the past once.

1 I _____ the washing up but then my boyfriend called. *(do)*

2 The new swimming pool _____ on March 1st but that doesn't look likely now. *(open)*

3 I'm surprised. I never thought he _____ it. *(finish)*

4 I _____ on getting my hair cut today but I've just changed my mind. *(plan)*

Quantifiers → 4B

2 Complete the chart with these words.

> a few   hardly any   a larger number of   several

Use quantifiers to tell you how much there is of a thing or things.	
LOTS OF ↓	loads of work / ᵃ_____ people plenty of time ᵇ_____ days a bit of work / ᶜ_____ friends ᵈ_____ sugar
NONE	no

Note the difference between *little* (=not much) and *a little* (= some).
I can't help you. I've got very little time today. / *I can help you. I've got a little time.*

3 <s>Cross out</s> the wrong word.

1 If you want another tea or coffee, help yourself. We've got *plenty of / a few* milk.

2 There are *several / little* different ways of getting from the airport to the city centre. Two or three, in fact.

3 We don't need to go to the supermarket. We've got *several / loads of* bread left.

4 I put *little / a little* chilli in the sauce so it's a bit spicy!

5 I'll be with you in a minute. I just need to answer *a few / hardly any* emails first.

The passive → 4C

Form the passive voice with verb *be* + past participle. Use *by* + the agent (doer) of the action. Use the passive:	
1 to focus on the object	The book **was written by** Paolo Coelho.
2 for actions when it's obvious who did it (e.g. the police, a hospital)	He **was given** some pretty strong medicine.
3 to describe a process	Most meat **is cooked** before we eat it.

4 Rewrite in the passive.

1 The government changed the law.
_____

2 A virus had infected my computer.
_____

3 They're opening the doors now.
_____

4 They've sent an email to all the students.
_____

4

Mixed conditionals →4D

5 Match the rules with the sentences.

1	The second conditional describes a purely hypothetical situation.	a	If I'**d gone** to the party last night, I'**d be feeling** terrible today.
2	The third conditional describes a hypothetical situation in the past.	b	If I **were** a billionaire, I'**d buy** my own island.
3	A mixed conditional looks at a hypothetical situation in the past, and a hypothetical result in the present.	c	If you'**d been** at the party last night, you'**d have had** a great time.

Adverbs and comparisons → 4E

6 Complete with *far* and *slightly*.

	Use adverbs with the comparative to mean *a lot* or *a little* more.
a lot	My mum's parents are **much older** than my dad's. The earrings are ᵃ_____ **more expensive** than the necklace.
a little	I think your Turkish is a **bit better** than mine. Our new apartment is ᵇ_____ **smaller** than our old one.

7 Complete with these words.

1. Your test results are _____ than the rest of the class. (much / bad)
2. The bus is _____ than driving. (slightly / cheap)
3. My sister's _____ than me. (bit / tall)
4. This year's exams were _____ than last year's. (far / difficult)

8 Read the rules. Then complete the examples with the missing words.

Compare two things with (*not*) *as* (adjective or adverb) *as*.	Joe isn't ¹_____ **fun as** Kalyan.
Nowhere near as and *not nearly as* mean 'absolutely not equal'.	But then Kalyan **is nowhere** ²_____ **as crazy as** Bill. He'll do anything!
just as… as means 'exactly equal'.	And Bill's brother is ³_____ **as mad as** him. Those two are unbelievable!
(*not*) *quite as* means 'almost'	On balance, I think I'd rather go out with Joe . An evening with him **isn't** ⁴_____ **as dangerous as** a night out with the others!

Linking phrases → 4F

There are a number of different words that you can use to structure a text. Although the words often express a similar meaning, they have different grammar.

1. Use **however** or **nevertheless** to compare whole sentences.
2. Use **although** or **even though** to link two clauses together in a single sentence.
3. Use **all in all** or **to sum up** to begin a new sentence, and to explain to the reader how the text works.

9 Read the rules 1–3. Circle the correct option.

1. We didn't have tickets for the festival. *Although / Nevertheless*, we decided to go there anyway.
2. So that's the end of my presentation. *However / To sum up*, we have discovered something very interesting.
3. We're working desperately to save these endangered species *even though / however* we don't have much hope for the future.

Answer key (inverted):

1 I was going to do 2 was to open 3 would finish 4 was planning
2 a a large number of b several c a few d hardly any
3 Correct words are: 1 plenty of 2 several 3 loads of 4 a little 5 a few
4 1 The law was changed (by the government). 2 My computer had been infected by a virus. 3 The doors are being opened now. 4 An email has been send to all the students.
5 1 b 2 c 3 a
6 a far b slightly
7 1 much worse 2 slightly cheaper 3 a bit taller 4 far more difficult
8 1 as much 2 near 3 just 4 quite
9 1 Nevertheless 2 To sum up 3 even though

119

Richmond Publishing
58 St Aldates
Oxford
OX1 1ST

© Richmond Publishing, 2010

ISBN: 978-84-668-1857-5

All rights reserved. No part of this book may be reproduced, stored in a retrieval system or transmitted in any form by any means, electronic, mechanical, photocopying, recording or otherwise, without the prior permission in writing of the publisher.

Printed by: *Orymu, S.A.*
D.L. M-21894-2011

Project Development: Sarah Thorpe
Editing: Sarah Thorpe and Rhona Snelling
Design and Layout: Nigel Jordan, Lorna Heaslip
Cover Design: Aqueduct, London and Richmond Publishing
Photo Research: Magdalena Mayo
Audio Production: Ian Harker

Many thanks to all the wonderful editorial and publishing team at Richmond for their collective creative efforts and hard work throughout, and to Carmen, Lula and Calum for putting up with so many hours of the back of my head – yet again.
(Paul Seligson)

Alastair Lane would like to thank Yvonne Lane, Sarah Thorpe, Rhona Snelling and the whole team at Richmond for their support and encouragement during the writing of this book.

Every effort has been made to trace the holders of copyright before publication. The publishers will be pleased to rectify any error or omission at the earliest opportunity.

Illustrations:
David Banks, Matt Buckley, Sarah Goodreau, Phil Hackett, Roger Harris, Matt Latchford, Ben Swift, Sam Wilson

Photographs:
C. Villalba; J. Jaime; Prats i Camps; S. Enríquez;
A. G. E. FOTOSTOCK; ACI AGENCIA DE FOTOGRAFÍA/ Alamy Images; COMSTOCK; CORDON PRESS/CORBIS/ George Hammerstein; FOTONONSTOP; GETTY IMAGES SALES SPAIN/Nick Yapp, Image Source, Ellinor Hall, Noah Clayton, David Lees, Antenna, Janet Kimber, SSPL, Anthony Lee, Sharon Dominick, Tim Graham, Paul Harris, Chase Jarvis, The Image Bank/Peter Adams, Hans Neleman, De Agostini/ G. Dagli Orti/DEA, ULTRA.F, AFP, Paul Nicklen, AFP/ Jack Guez, Carsten Koall, Somos/Veer, AFP/Yuri Yuriev, Rob Atkins, Digital Vision, David De Lossy, Altrendo Images, David Silverman, Hiroshi Higuchi, Joan White, David Young-Wolff, AFP/Andrea Bambino, AFP/ Antonio Scorza, Christopher Pillitz, Dimitri Vervitsiotis, Wirelmage/Jesse Grant, José Luis Pelaez, Inc., Paul Bradbury, Bloomberg via/Andrew Harrer, Melissa and Jackson Brandts, Keystone Features/John Pratt, Dougal Waters, Time Life Pictures/Pix Inc./Jacqueline Paul, Glowimages; HIGHRES PRESS STOCK/AbleStock.com; I. Preysler; ISTOCKPHOTO; MUSEUM ICONOGRAFÍA/ *J. Martin*; Rex Features/John Alex Maguire; Rex Features/ Action Press; Rex Features/Channel 4; Rex Features/Everett; Rex Features/Newspix/J. Durrans; Rex Features; MATTON-BILD; Photos.com Plus; ARCHIVO SANTILLANA; Maynard Farrell; Desmond Morris; Hog Wild LLC; Telegraph Media Group Limited/ Clara Molden; Jobar International; Grey Group; TU Berlin; RDF Television